Feasting
on the
Words of
Christ

"Let your soul delight itself in fatness"

• • •

Melanie Stroud

Feasting on the Words of Christ
Copyright © 2022 by Melanie Stroud. All rights reserved.

This material is neither made, provided, approved, nor endorsed by Intellectual Reserve, Inc. or The Church of Jesus Christ of Latter-day Saints. Any content or opinions expressed, implied or included in or with the material are solely those of the owner and not those of Intellectual Reserve, Inc. or The Church of Jesus Christ of Latter-day Saints.

For privacy reasons, some names, locations, and dates may have been changed.

ISBN: 978-1-7376986-3-0 (Paperback)
ISBN: 978-1-7376986-4-7 (Ebook)

Design by Miblart.com
Editing by Blair Parke

E n' S Publishing

In Memory of
Curtis P. Wilson
President of the Kobe, Japan Mission
from
1992—1995

"... feast upon the words of Christ; for behold, the words of Christ will tell you all things what ye should do."
(2 Nephi 32:3)

TABLE OF CONTENTS

PART 2

INTRODUCTION

I like donuts. Ok, I *love* donuts. I want to eat them all the time. If there is a donut that is available to be eaten, I will eat it. I have no willpower whatsoever when it comes to this type of pastry.

Over the course of my life, donuts have become my go-to. When I'm feeling sad, donut time. When I am going through a rough patch, donut time. Saturday morning donuts? Yes! It's tradition. *The kids want donuts. They are not for me. They are for the kids. I must go get them.*

There is a place by my house called Sunrise Donuts. This place makes the best donuts. They are to die for. Their maple bars and strawberry-iced donuts are the best. I'm drooling as I reminisce.

Years back, in my first marriage, I would go there all the time. (I still do, shh, but that's irrelevant.) I would buy my donuts with my credit card on their little Apple Pay machine. Unbeknownst to me, my apple account was somehow connected to my husband's account, and every time I would buy some donuts, he'd get a text with the receipt. When I found out, I was so embarrassed. How long had he been getting the alert every time I bought one? My secret pleasure really wasn't a secret? No! But did knowing that fact stop me from going to the donut shop?

Don't be crazy. I just made sure I had cash on hand going forward. I was not about to buy a donut on credit. No way. Cash only. The madness continued.

I'm laughing as I write this, and a bead of sweat just ran down my back as the thought creeps into my mind. *He's not still getting those alerts, right? I really did fix that, right? Oh, please bless I fixed that.*

Sadly, something bad has happened. All these years of donuts put me on the verge of diabetes. I'm points away; I'm not healthy. My body is screaming at me to shape up, get moving, and start putting healthy food into my face. The writing on the wall can no longer be denied. All those donuts, in fact, did me dirty. These donuts didn't keep me thin. These donuts helped raise my cholesterol and have not helped my heart. I have to find a way to stop. It's the pits. I'm really sad about it.

Over the years, I have also developed another habit. It's like turning to donuts, but I have been turning to the word of God. When I'm feeling sad, scripture time. When I'm going through a rough patch, scripture time. I've also done all I can to try to get my kids to turn to the scriptures and make reading them a tradition in their lives as well. I know how delicious feasting on the words of Christ can become and know how delicious the words of Christ are to me. I don't want to go even a few days without them.

When I do, I notice I start feeling sad or angry or just out of sorts. Small things feel too large, and I get discouraged and confused. Finally, the fog will lift, and I'll think, *Doy, you haven't turned to the scriptures. Your soul is starving!*

Do you remember that hilarious skit from *Saturday Night Live* where Chris Farley and some other cast members are dressed like women who are out to lunch? Chris starts eating some of his friend's French fries, and his friend reminds him that he probably shouldn't eat them because isn't he trying to lose weight? Chris turns and says in a scary voice, "Lay off me! I'm starving." He almost sounds possessed, and it makes me laugh so hard. I repeat those words in that scary possessed voice so often, "Lay off me. I'm starving!"

I imagine that's what my soul says when I've neglected my study for too long. When it does, I have to listen. The best thing about starving souls is that we can shove them so full of goodness and they never get wrecked by it. The opposite is true. Instead of a weakened heart filled with pastry fat, we can grow a ginormous heart that changes our very nature.

Feasting on spiritual food doesn't slow us down but propels us forward. We're ready to not only listen to the Lord but act in His name. Feasting on the words of Christ really is so much fun and has become delicious to me.

When I was a twenty-one-year-old missionary in Japan, almost thirty years ago, I was taught a five-step method for studying the Book of Mormon and the scriptures. There is nothing revolutionary about the steps; we've heard them before—they include search, ponder, and pray. But there's something about doing it the way I learned, which includes pondering and writing, being grateful, and repenting, that really changes the game. Studying this way, you can learn to hear the Savior's voice speaking directly to you as you take the time to turn to Him each day in the word of God. It's the best thing ever. It's a miracle.

I've tried to write this book for almost thirty years. It's such an important message, and I've beat myself up for years that I haven't yet written it all down. But as I sit here, finally getting this all on paper, I realize why I had to wait so long. This book had to include the *result* of over twenty-five years of studying this way. I had to really look and see what this program did for me, and hundreds of others, over the long haul. What happened as a result of all this soul-feasting?

Upon investigation, I learned a fundamental truth. Reading the Book of Mormon and searching His word every day brought me to Jesus Christ.

Through almost thirty years of regularly studying the Book of Mormon this way, I've learned to hear Christ's voice when I read the scriptures. I recognize it and feel Him near so often.

There is a beautiful scripture in the New Testament where Jesus compares His followers to sheep. He says, "My sheep hear my voice, and I know them, and they follow me" (John 10:27). *This* is what has happened to me. I recognize His voice. I have learned that Christ knows me, He wants to lead and direct me, and He can do this very clearly and simply. I treasure this knowledge more than any donut or anything else! It's the one thing that brings me joy on a daily basis. Jesus Christ has become my friend.

It can happen to you. It *will* happen to you if you take the time to study the Book of Mormon every day, as I am about to show you. I promise.

Who am I besides some lady who loves donuts and Jesus? I'm a mother of five homegrown kids and three step-kids. I'm married to the most amazing man that I met at a family reunion in Alabama. I love that we met that way. It's always so funny to say. Don't worry, we aren't blood relatives. I graduated from Brigham Young University with a degree in special education and served as a missionary in Japan. I own a car and pay utilities. Blah blah. Basically, I'm just like you, just a normal person. I don't have advanced degrees in religious studies or ancient Hebrew. I'm just a girl that eats too many donuts and loves the scriptures so much. I'm also a podcast host and now a writer.

In November 2019, I had the very distinct impression that I needed to share my testimony with the world. It was a neat thought, but how? As I tumbled that idea around a bit, a friend suggested I start a podcast. That sounded interesting, but I had no idea how to do it.

I had recently started listening to KSL's *Cold* podcast, a Salt Lake City-based podcast about the disappearance and possible murder of Susan Powell by her husband, Josh, and what happened after her disappearance. And that's all I knew about podcasts. Clearly, I didn't have anything that exciting to say—no murder or intrigue. Who would listen?

But to make a very long story short, I started a podcast at the beginning of 2019 that followed The Church of Jesus Christ of Latter-Day Saints' new *Come Follow Me* weekly curriculum. For the last four years, I've been teaching and testifying about the beautiful stories in the Bible, the Book of Mormon, and throughout church history. But it seems like I always circle back to the power of the Book of Mormon. I challenge people all the time to put their faces in the Book of Mormon every day. I created a stand-alone episode about the power of the Book of Mormon and have sent people to it again and again.

When people begin to study the Book of Mormon this way, marvelous things happen. Lives change. People whose testimonies were dwindling come back to the faith. People who were completely out have returned, and countless prayers have been answered.

President Russel M. Nelson recently warned, "...in coming days, it will not be possible to survive spiritually without the guiding, directing, comforting, and constant influence of the Holy Ghost." He then pleaded, "...I plead with you to increase your spiritual capacity to receive revelation."[1] Studying the Book of Mormon like this every day is a key way to receive this desperately needed revelation and direction.

I can't trust that someone will just stumble upon my podcast and find that one episode any longer. I can't wait to get invited to another Stake Fireside and hope the right people hear this truth. It's so important this message reaches as many people as quickly as possible. Time is running out. Satan is waging his final battle, and he's looking to pull each of us away from the God we love. We need the protection and guidance of the Holy Ghost in our lives every day if we hope to make it back to our Heavenly Father and Jesus Christ to live with them on a forever basis. Protection, guidance, and so much more are available to all of us.

Come, let me teach you how to better feast on Christ's words and on His love.

> Come ... every one that thirsteth come ye to the waters and he that hath no money come buy and eat; yea, come buy ... without money and without price.
>
> ... come unto the Holy One of Israel, and feast upon that which perisheth not, neither can be corrupted, and let your soul delight in fatness (2 Nephi 9:50-51).

PART 1

CHAPTER 1

"There is a power in the book which will begin to flow into your lives the moment you begin a serious study of the book. You will find greater power to resist temptation. You will find the power to avoid deception. You will find the power to stay on the strait and narrow path."

President Ezra Taft Benson

Growing up, my family had a modest home with a pool and a playhouse in the backyard. We went to California and Utah for vacations every year. Our cars ran well, and we had plenty of food. My father was a custom jeweler who owned his own business for most of his life. My mom stayed home while we were all little and returned to teaching high school when my youngest brother went to kindergarten.

While we certainly had enough money, we were not what most people consider rich. There were six kids in my family, and my mom could really stretch a dollar. She was the queen of getting things at yard sales and on sale. Her talent for finding bargains helped a lot with the family budget.

Back then, there was a store called Mervyn's; I think you could compare it to something like Kohl's today. They would have these big sales once a month and people would line up outside before they opened to then rush in and get the bargains. There was even a commercial that aired for a while that showed a woman standing outside the store, looking excitedly inside the locked glass door while chanting, "Open. Open. Open."

My mom was just like the lady in the commercial. She was addicted! She still brags, to this day, that she had a baby on a Tuesday and still made it to the Mervyn's sale on Friday. The result of those sales was that our clothes were just fine, but not expensive. When I was younger, it hadn't really mattered much to me. But when I entered high school, as a freshman, things changed a little. I began to notice and care.

Our high school was a weird melting pot of neighborhoods. We had very wealthy kids who drove expensive cars, lived in huge houses behind a guard gate, and wore all the modern, costly clothes. And to the opposite extreme, we had some very inexpensive apartments that housed kids who barely had anything. My family sat somewhere in the middle of that dichotomy.

Because of this economic gap, the contrast in social classes was pretty apparent at school. Admittedly, I was jealous that I didn't have more money or fancier clothes. But also, some not-so-nice girls found multiple opportunities at school to drive the point home. They were like the popular kids in most 1980s flicks that always made everyone around them feel small and unimportant. The words they often said and the message that their clothes screamed at me was, "You are not cool because you don't wear the right clothes."

As I started my freshman year, I began going to seminary—a church class that most Latter-day Saint high-schoolers worldwide take every day of the school week.

The course of study that year was the Book of Mormon. Our teacher gave us a challenge with a reward. If we read the Book of Mormon every day throughout the year, we would get this little gold pendant. The pendant was an open book that said, "Moroni's Promise" on it. Because my dad was a jeweler, he agreed to make them for everyone who fulfilled the challenge. Everyone else would get a gold-plated one, but not me—my dad said he would make mine in real 14K gold!

I swear I felt like Gollum in the *Lord of the Rings*. "Come to me, my precious." I couldn't stop thinking about the necklace. I'm not sure why I wanted it so badly, but I had to have it.

Thus, every night I would read the Book of Mormon before bed. I even got a non-member friend to check in on me at night to ensure I was diligent. I was serious.

President Thomas S. Monson described the real prize for reading the Book of Mormon every day when he promised that by doing so, we "... will be in a position to hear the voice of the Spirit, to resist temptation, to overcome doubt and fear, and to receive heaven's help in our lives."[2] But that was an obscure carrot to dangle over a young teenager. The promise of the pendant was enough to get me started. I began to read every night before bed.

One particular day, a group of popular girls chose to look down their noses at me for the umpteenth time because I didn't have a little triangle on the back of my jeans. That, you see, was the symbol for GUESS® jeans. And in the eighties, anyone who was anyone wore GUESS® clothes. Don't forget—while my mom did all she could to outfit us well, we weren't going to Dillard's and buying $50 jeans. It just wasn't happening.

That day, these girls had been pretty rude to me and had made me feel uncool and small. I'm sure it was a mix of their meanness and my envy that had me feeling pretty down that night as I settled in to read the scriptures before I got in bed.

I opened my Book of Mormon to read for the night. I didn't look up GUESS® clothes, envy, or mean girls in the topical guide. I just opened right to where I was. I was in Jacob, chapter two, where it said:

> And the hand of providence hath smiled upon you most pleasingly, that you have obtained many riches; and because some of you have obtained more abundantly than that of your brethren ye are lifted up in the pride of your hearts, and wear stiff necks and high heads because of the costliness of your apparel, and persecute your brethren because ye suppose that ye are better than they (Jacob 2:13).

These words were no longer just words on a page about people long, long ago. No. This story was about me—about what I had experienced that very day. The words didn't just feel like a nice, little coincidence. The moment I read them, I was filled with an unmistakable rush of the Spirit. Those words were carried into my heart and landed there with such a crash that I'm surprised my siblings didn't hear it in their rooms upstairs. The Lord was there, and He was speaking to me through the text of scripture accompanied by the power of the Holy Ghost.

I can't sufficiently explain what this moment did for me. I suddenly learned that the Creator of the universe, the very God of heaven and earth, knew me. He cared that I cared about GUESS® jeans. My sadness was over something so small. It really wasn't a big deal. But I learned that night that whatever was a big deal to me was a big deal to Him—and that's a big deal.

As I continued to read, a few verses later, it said, "But before ye seek for riches, seek ye for the kingdom of God" (Jacob 2:18).

Not only did I learn that Heavenly Father and Jesus Christ knew me and were aware of my situation, but I also learned that I needed to have my eyes set on the things of God more than the things of the world. I learned so much that night from just two verses in the Book of Mormon.

That experience was one of the best gifts I ever received from heaven. I count it as such a blessing because it happened when I was *so young*. What a gift to give a thirteen-year-old. I can't think of a better way to lay the foundation of a faith-filled life than to speak to a teenager so specifically that she knew it came from God.

I want to convey this fact to you in the most straightforward way possible. When the Lord reaches out to you through the pages of scripture it is often accompanied by what I call a whoosh of the Spirit. You don't have to guess if the Lord is trying to teach you something; you will know.

The prophet Joseph Smith shared his account of reading the Bible while pondering which church to join. He explained his experience with getting an answer through the scriptures like this: "Never did any passage of scripture come with more power to the heart of man than this did at this time to mine. It seemed to enter with great force into every feeling of my heart."[3]

This is what happened to me. God's message came to me, accompanied by an overwhelming presence of the Spirit. I felt the Spirit whisper, "I see you, Melanie. I know of your troubles. I care about what you care about."

If you polled the general membership of The Church of Jesus Christ of Latter-day Saints and asked them what the first miracle of the restoration was, I am ninety-eight percent sure they would say, "The First Vision." That's where it all started, right? That is where Joseph Smith got the answer to his prayer. In that grove, he learned that God the Father and his Son, Jesus Christ, are real. It was there he learned that he would have a hand in bringing Christ's original church back to the earth. It was amazing. The heavens had opened again. His prayer was answered.

But as amazing as that event was, I don't think it was any more amazing than what happened to Joseph Smith in his house when he was reading the Bible.

What inspired Joseph to go to the grove and ask what church to join? The message he got from his Father in Heaven *from the Bible*. Heavenly Father spoke to him through the pages of the Bible *before* He ever conversed with him in person in the grove. That, to me, is the first real miracle of the restoration.

Because God can speak so clearly to us through the pages of scripture, we too can *feel* answers like Joseph did—*in every feeling of our hearts*. This is because of the power of the Holy Ghost.

In the Doctrine and Covenants, it says:

> Yea, behold, I will tell you in your mind and in your heart, by the Holy Ghost, which shall come upon you and which shall dwell in your heart. Now, behold, this is the Spirit of revelation; behold, this is the Spirit by which Moses brought the children of Israel through the Red Sea on dry ground (Doctrine and Covenants 6:8-10).

Remember when the Israelites were following Moses and escaping out of Egypt? Remember when they got to the Red Sea, and it looked like they were trapped? What did the Lord do for them? He parted the Red Sea. It was truly miraculous. Everyone who was there knew that something impossible had just happened, I'm sure.

This scripture in the Doctrine and Covenants teaches that the same Spirit that parted the Red Sea is the Spirit that will teach you and me what is true. It is the Spirit of revelation that all of us can receive in our minds and hearts as we seek it.

Do you understand the weight of this? This *discernable power* provided by the Holy Ghost is why people give up everything to join the church. This same power is why pioneer ancestors crossed seas and plains, enduring unimaginable hardships to follow the Lord in these Latter-days. They felt something more substantial than a "good feeling." They didn't just believe the missionaries or want to gather with people for fun or because this church taught some nice things. They stood on the shores of their personal Red Seas and watched them part. And because of the enormity of that confirmation of the Spirit, they moved to act.

President Ezra Taft Benson said the following:

> There is a power in the book which will begin to flow into your lives the moment you begin a serious study of the book. You will find greater power to resist temptation. You will find the power to avoid deception. You will find the power to stay on the strait and narrow path.[4]

I testify with all my heart his words are true. The experiences I have had hearing the voice of the Lord and feeling the whoosh of the Spirit as I have read the Book of Mormon have changed my life. My experiences have helped me avoid deception and have kept me safe. My experiences have brought me closer to my Savior. I am so thankful for this gift in my life.

The Book of Mormon begins with a powerful promise in the introduction:

> We invite all men everywhere to read the Book of Mormon, to ponder in their hearts the message it contains, and then to ask God, the Eternal Father, in the name of Christ if the book is true. Those who pursue this course and ask in faith will gain a testimony of its truth and divinity by the power of the Holy Ghost (See Moroni 10:3–5).

> Those who gain this divine witness from the Holy Spirit will also come to know by the same power that Jesus Christ is the Savior of the world, that Joseph Smith is His revelator and prophet in these last days, and that The Church of Jesus Christ of Latter-day Saints is the Lord's kingdom once again established on the earth, preparatory to the Second Coming of the Messiah.[5]

Wow. That's powerful. Those are some hefty promises. And this promise is another reason to begin this study. So many questions can be answered, and doubts laid to rest, by immersing yourself in the Book of Mormon each day.

CHAPTER 2

*"...there was also written upon them a new
writing, which was plain to be read, which did
give us understanding concerning the ways of
the Lord; and it was written and changed from
time to time, according to the faith and diligence
which we gave unto it."*

1 Nephi 16:29

It's no coincidence that the Book of Mormon started with an imperfect family. Immediately, we can
relate. They have their share of trouble. Sure, the
dad was a prophet and got direct counsel from God
a lot. But even some of the prophet's kids were bratty
and hard to handle. They fought. They complained.
They even tried to kill each other. The mom nagged
the dad. The prophet even started complaining when
he was hungry; and, at one point, Mom and Dad get
so fed up that they went to the bottom of their boat
and wished to die. Really. They would rather perish
than deal with their jerk kids any longer.

But the greatest part is even in all their imperfec-
tion, we learn so many important lessons from them.

They gave us hope. They helped us see how often the Lord is willing to forgive and give us another chance. We see the power of God and what it can do to soften hearts. They experienced miracles even when they screwed up time and time again. We see the power of a good example and the faith it takes to keep returning to God when things are hard. I love Lehi and his family and the things I've learned from them over the years.

For those not familiar with the Book of Mormon, I'll give you a tiny bit of backstory to bring you up to speed. At the beginning of the book, the Lord tells Lehi, the dad and prophet, that Jerusalem is going to be destroyed, and he needs to take his family and leave town. But they don't get to go buy a new house in another city. They have to leave most of their possessions behind, grab some tents, and head off into the wilderness. Not fun.

But they obey. Lehi and his family follow the Lord's direction and leave Jerusalem. Some exciting stuff happens that you're going to have to read about on your own, like Lehi's sons being commanded to go back to town to get some records from this rich guy, and the rich guy ends up losing his head. Nephi, the super righteous son, puts on the dead guy's bloody clothes and goes back to his brothers. They think it's the bad guy. It's quite exciting.

Then after they get all the way back to their dad in the wilderness with the records, the boys are told they have to go back to town and get some women to marry. It was kind of like the ever-popular 1950's musical, *Seven Brides for Seven Brothers*. But they don't steal the girls and then cause an avalanche that stops the rescue of those sobbing women. They get permission. Actually, come to think of it, it's not really like that movie at all. I guess I just like to imagine that return trip being a little more exciting than just walking back to camp in the burning sun and having an uncomfortable conversation about the weather.

But after all that, they are in the wilderness, wandering, searching for food, and, apparently, their women are getting really buff. But now what? What are they supposed to do next?

One morning they wake up, and a "ball of curious workmanship" (1 Nephi 16:10) is sitting outside their tent. It is called the Liahona, and it is given to them by God. We are told that there are two spindles in it, and one of the spindles points in the direction they should go. How handy, an older version of GPS.

Nephi then explains that they follow the pointers, and the Liahona leads them to the most fertile hunting grounds. It really helps a lot.

But then Nephi breaks his bow, and everyone starts murmuring. And let's cut them some slack. I say and do things when I'm hungry that I'm not always proud of. These guys are hangry! While everyone is whining and moaning about their situation, ever-diligent Nephi goes and fixes his bow, and then comes back and asks his dad to ask the Lord where he should go to find food. Lehi then humbles himself, gets a little chastening from the Lord for his attitude, and is told to look at the ball.

I wonder here if they had forgotten about it. When the bow broke, we know they didn't go to the Liahona for guidance. Why not? Lehi knows he has this tool; it worked in the past. Why didn't he go straight to it?

Well, for starters, he was hungry, and he had a bunch of whiny kids. Just raising two of his kids, Laman and Lemuel, was a constant battle, I'm sure.

So, the first reason I see why they didn't turn to the Liahona for direction was *they were distracted. They were busy.* Life gets busy. That tent couldn't sweep itself out every morning. The camels needed watering, and Laman and Lemuel needed constant attention. There was a lot to do every single day.

Next, the Liahona was *new.* They hadn't used it for very long, so they didn't know all it could do for them. So far, the spindles had led them where to go, and that was about it. When this problem arose with the broken bow, they didn't think they needed the Liahona. They had stopped moving, so no need for directions yet, right?

After Lehi's chastening from the Lord for complaining right along with his kids, the Lord commands him to *go to the ball.*

"... Look upon the ball, and behold the things which are written" (1 Nephi 16:26).

I wonder if they thought, *Written on the ball? Wait, what? We thought it was just spindles, spinning.*

Someone then goes to the tent and digs it out from under a saddle or the pile of shirts that need to be washed.

"And it came to pass that when my father beheld the things which were written upon the ball, he did fear and tremble exceedingly, and also my brethren and the sons of Ishmael and our wives" (1 Nephi 16:27).

Why did they fear and tremble? Because "there was also written upon them a new writing, which was plain to be read, which did give us understanding concerning the ways of the Lord; and it was written and changed from time to time, according to the faith and diligence which we gave unto it" (1 Nephi 16:29).

I have always wondered about the mechanism here. Was it digital? Did they get something like text messages from heaven? That would make you fear and tremble if all you were used to was writing on heavy scrolls or words carved into metal plates. Were different words etched into the ball every time they turned to it with faith? Either way, it was astonishing enough that it made them tremble.

Nephi talks about how everyone's minds were blown—except his. It just says that he followed the directions written on the ball up to the top of a mountain. There he was able to find food for his family.

At this time, Nephi also makes this crucial observation. He notices that the Liahona only worked when they had faith it would work and when they were diligent about turning to it.

It also works better when they *do* what they read or see. Nephi sees where to go and goes straight there. While the others are oohing and ahhing about the message, Nephi is heading to the mountain.

President Nelson was talking with a group of kids in April of 2020, and one kid asked him, "Is it hard being the prophet?"

I loved President Nelson's reply:

Everything to do with becoming more like the Savior is difficult. For example, when God wanted to give the Ten Commandments to Moses, where did He tell Moses to go? Up on top of a mountain, on the top of Mount Sinai. So Moses had to walk all the way up to the top of that mountain to get the Ten Commandments. Now, Heavenly Father could have said, "Moses, you start there, and I'll start here, and I'll meet you halfway." No, the Lord loves effort, because effort brings rewards that can't come without it.[6]

All the many, many times I have read this account of Nephi and the broken bow, I had missed that Nephi was commanded to go to the top of a mountain to find food. The Lord could have said, "Good job, guys, for humbling yourselves and finally looking at the ball again. It's all good. Turn around. Is that a deer I think I see in the thicket behind you?"

But the fact that Nephi had to follow the directions and head to the top of the mountain is such an essential part of the story. Nephi had to believe that what the ball said was really coming from the Lord. He had to believe to the point of climbing a high mountain before the Lord gave him the food. He had to have faith and diligence to make the ball work, and then he had to DO what it said to solidify the truthfulness of the message and the power of the ball. He could have second-guessed it or decided to talk it out with his siblings. "Is the top of the mountain the best place to look for deer?"

But he didn't. He went and did what it said right away. This is Nephi, our go-and-do guy. He's the man who said:

I will go and do the things which the Lord
hath commanded, for I know that the Lord
giveth no commandments unto the children of
men, save he shall prepare a way for them that
they may accomplish the thing which he com-
mandeth them (1 Nephi 3:7).

Nephi is a doer.

We see the result of following the spindles and the
words written on the ball and getting to the top of
the mountain—he finds the food and brings it to his
family.

Shortly after I was married to my first husband,
we were preparing to move from Utah to Virginia
for my husband to start his post-graduate schooling.
We didn't have a lot of money and were trying to
figure out just how to get our stuff out there. We
had been praying that all would go smoothly as we
made our move to the East Coast.

That month before we were to leave, we got
a check in the mail from my grandfather. It was
strange because he wasn't the guy that sent checks—
we never got gifts unless it was Christmas or our
birthdays. But somehow, the Lord had whispered to
him that we needed a little extra, and he sent us
some. Things were looking up. We were excited to
start this next phase of our lives.

Not long after that, my husband came to me worried about his little sister. She needed some money,
and he wanted to know if we could give her some.
Looking back, the amount was so small, and I'm embarrassed this was even a thing. But funds were so

tight. I really didn't think we had enough to give. I told him I wasn't sure.

That night, I opened my Book of Mormon to read for the day. I was in the book of Mosiah, chapter four, when I came to verse twenty-one and stopped. I couldn't believe it. It said:

> And now, if God, who has created you, on whom you are dependent for your lives and for all that ye have and are, doth grant unto you whatsoever ye ask that is right, in faith, believing that ye shall receive, *O then, how ye ought to impart of the substance that ye have one to another* (Mosiah 4:21 emphasis added).

I had read that verse plenty of times throughout my life. But that night, the words took on new meaning. That night, the Book of Mormon was like my own personal Liahona. The writing changed, as the spindles pointed the way I should go. The Lord said directly to my heart, through the power of the Holy Ghost, "Remember that money I just sent you, because you'd been asking for it? I think you need to share some of it."

I didn't have to look up 'selfish sister-in-law' in the topical guide. I didn't even head to the Book of Mormon looking for an answer to this problem. I went to it because it had become a habit, and through that little act of picking up "the ball," I was led to what I needed to do. I felt like Lehi's family when they trembled exceedingly after it told them where to hunt for food. The message was so direct! It wasn't a coincidence. The Lord had told me through the pages of holy scripture what I needed to do.

When President Benson said that there was power in the Book of Mormon, he wasn't kidding. I've seen this power time and time again. The Book of Mormon is like our own personal Liahona. But like Lehi discovered, it only works when we diligently turn to it with faith.

Lehi and his family make it through the wilderness and end up on the seashore. They are then commanded to build a boat to sail across the sea. Just the fact that they even learned how to build a boat is a miracle. I wonder if the Liahona worked much like YouTube during this process. "No, turn that part around. It will never seal if it's backward like that." So fun to think about, right?

Well, they build a boat, it floats, and Laman and Lemuel are impressed. Then they all set out across the sea.

After many days, Laman, Lemuel, and some of Ishmael's kids start singing and dancing, being rude and forgetting how they got to where they were.

Nephi then gets worried that the Lord will stop helping them and tries to make them stop.

I feel bad for Nephi. He is their little brother, and he always ends up being the one to try to get them to follow God. I'm sure it wasn't a fun place to be. We learn from the story of Joseph and his *amazing technicolor dream-coat* that older brothers don't always love younger brothers telling them what to do. Little brothers, being the righteous favorites, don't always get along well with rebellious older brothers. But since they are on a boat, and Laman and Lemuel can't sell Nephi to some passing Ishmaelites, they tie him up instead.

"Leave us alone, bro. We can say whatever we want, and we're sick of you telling us what to do!"

As soon as they tie him up, the Liahona stops working, and a storm comes. They are getting all tossed around and don't know where to go or how to steer.

They let this nightmare go on for four whole days.

Why?

Once again, they know that the Liahona is the key. Why didn't they just apologize, untie Nephi, and turn back to the ball?

As day four is wrapping up, the storm is so bad that they think they will perish. I'm sure everyone had been puking off the side of the boat for days and begging to untie Nephi. Finally, Laman and Lemuel agree and untie him.

What does Nephi do at this point?

He goes straight to the compass. Straight. To. The. Compass. He knows it is the key to their survival. He knows the power it has to guide their journey.

He then prays, the compass starts working, the storm ceases, and there is *a great calm* (1 Nephi 18:21).

They continue their journey, and a little while later, with Nephi guiding the ship, they make it to the promised land.

Do you need your storm to cease? Are you yearning for a great calm? There's a powerful lesson to be learned about what this gift did for Lehi and his family.

If we continue reading the Book of Mormon, the Liahona is referred to once more in-depth. Another prophet, named Alma, is explaining to his son Helaman how important it is that they keep special care of the records of their people. The records that he is talking about are the gold plates that later become the Book of Mormon. It is of the very utmost importance. Alma is about to give these plates to Helaman, and Helaman can't slack on this one.

I don't know why I like to retell the stories in my voice—maybe because when you add thees and thous, sometimes people tune out. Maybe I like doing it because I imagine these people as real people, just like you and me, having real conversations.

Alma's counsel to Helaman pretty much went like this.

I received these records a long time ago and have kept them and added more. And the crazy thing is it almost seems foolish to believe that our lives and experiences will be so important to future generations. But they will be.

Here's how I know, Helaman, my boy. So far, these words, right here on these plates, have already convinced thousands of people of the errors of their ways and have brought them to Jesus Christ. In fact, these plates are precisely what Ammon and his brothers used when teaching the Lamanites, and it worked!! This record, somehow, brought all who would listen to it to the Savior, Jesus Christ. These words literally brought thousands of Lamanites to salvation.

Alma continues:

> *I still don't fully get it, but I know this record is crazy*
> *powerful, and it can change lives for the better. It is the*
> *means God uses to show forth His power unto people.*
> *I'm not exactly sure how it works, but I know it does*
> *because I've seen it happen again and again.*

Then Alma advises Helaman to "Counsel with the Lord in all thy doings" (Alma 37:37).

I've kind of become a word nerd lately. If you look up the word *counsel*, it means an "interchange of opinions, consultation; deliberation."[7] That sounds like *a conversation* to me. Alma is telling Helaman he needs to have conversations with the Lord. Saying a prayer *to* God isn't really an interchange. A prayer feels pretty one way to me. Alma said we need to *counsel* with the Lord.

Alma explains:

> And now, my son, I have somewhat to say con-
> cerning the thing which our fathers call a ball,
> or director—or our fathers called it Liahona,
> which is, being interpreted, a compass; and
> the Lord prepared it. ... And behold, it was
> prepared to show unto our fathers the course
> which they should travel in the wilderness. And
> it did work for them according to their faith
> in God; therefore, if they had faith to believe
> that God could cause that those spindles should
> point the way they should go, behold, it was
> done; therefore they had this miracle ... Nev-

ertheless, because those miracles were worked by small means it did show unto them marvelous works. They were slothful, and forgot to exercise their faith and diligence and then those marvelous works ceased, and they did not progress in their journey; Therefore, they tarried in the wilderness, or did not travel a direct course, and were afflicted with hunger and thirst, because of their transgressions. And now, my son, I would that ye should understand that these things are not without a shadow; for as our fathers were slothful to give heed to this compass (now these things were temporal) they did not prosper; even so it is with things which are spiritual (Alma 37:41).

Why did Lehi's family stop turning to the Liahona? Because it was *too easy*—too small a thing.

It reminds me of the story of Naaman in the Old Testament. He was a powerful captain to the king of Syria. The Bible says that he was an honorable, great guy, but there was a problem. He also had leprosy. Not fun.

Have you ever done one of those foot masks, where you put on those little, plastic booties that are filled with some kind of chemical liquid? You wear them for about an hour, and then like three days later, all your skin starts to peel off your feet. It takes about a week for it all to come off. It's really quite gross and is like a mild case of self-inflicted leprosy. Yuck.

Anyhoo, back to the story about Naaman—the guy with real leprosy—not the story of my crusty feet.

One day, one particular Israelite woman told the queen that there was a prophet who could probably heal Naaman if he could meet him. The queen got excited and told the king. The king then sent Naaman with money, clothes, horses, and a chariot to find this prophet. It reminds me of the scene in the ever-popular 1990's Disney cartoon *Aladdin*, where Aladdin shows up in Acrabah with his giant entourage. Naaman was coming like that—*he's a big deal.*

When Naaman finally showed up at the prophet Elijah's door, he told the servant of Elijah why he was there. Elijah sent down a message, "Go and wash in Jordan seven times, and thy flesh shall come again to thee, and thou shalt be clean" (2 Kings 5:10).

Easy enough.

But it wasn't easy, not to Big Deal Naaman. He was honorable and great, but *he knew* he was honorable and great and felt he wasn't being treated like the big deal that he thought he was.

He got really mad and left, saying to someone in his company, why didn't he "come out to me, and stand, and call on the name of the Lord his God, and strike his hand over the place, and recover the leper" (2 Kings 5:11). In essence, *That's it? He just told me to go wash in the Jordan? The Jordan? That's a filthy, little river. That's all?*

His servants let him simmer down, I suppose, and then, I imagine them awkwardly walking up, and after hemming and hawing and kicking the dirt around, someone said, "... if the prophet had bid thee do some great thing, wouldest thou not have done it? how much rather then, when he saith to thee, Wash, and be clean?" (2 Kings 5:13).

I'm not sure what changed Naaman's heart, but he agreed, humbled himself, went to the river, and did as he was told. With that, he was miraculously healed.

Why did Naaman initially refuse to do what the prophet told him to do? Because it was *too easy*.

Likewise, so many Israelites died after being bitten by poisonous serpents because they wouldn't look at the brass serpent on the pole that God had prepared to heal them (Num. 21). They didn't believe that looking would save them, so they didn't look and they died.

Why didn't they look? Because it was *too easy*. Surely some big result had to come from some big thing, right?

You would think, but in these aforementioned instances, doing something very small led to astounding results.

Each of us has been handed our own ball of curious workmanship at some point in our lives. It's the Book of Mormon. And if we want it to work for us as the Liahona worked for Lehi and his family, we have to make sure that we aren't making the same mistakes they did, and that we learn the important lessons that they learned.

1. We can't be too busy or distracted to find time to look into the word of Christ. We need to dust off the Book of Mormon and make time to look at it every single day.

2. We have to understand how the word works and the power that it has to change our very hearts and lives if we are diligent about turning to it.

3. We have to beware of pride. Pride will stop us from turning to God every time. We need to learn how desperately dependent we are on the Lord for our happiness on this journey. If we humbly turn to God when trials arise in our lives, then we can be led and guided to the promised land.

4. We have to do our best to keep the commandments and covenants and repent quickly when we don't. One of the fundamental keys to the Lord being able to use the Book of Mormon to lead our lives is that we need to be worthy to have the Spirit with us. The Lord speaks to us through the power of the Holy Ghost. Therefore, we have to do all we can to keep the Holy Ghost with us.

5. And last, many will say, "That can't be it. Just reading the Book of Mormon every day can't save me. No way. That's too easy."

Alma stated:

> For behold, it is as easy to give heed to the word of Christ, which will point to you a straight course to eternal bliss, as it was for our fathers to give heed to this compass, which would point unto them a straight course to the

promised land. ...For just as surely as this director did bring our fathers, by following its course, to the promised land, shall the words of Christ, if we follow their course, carry us beyond this vale of sorrow into a far better land of promise (Alma 37:44 emphasis added).

Alma promised Helaman that the words of Christ can *carry us beyond this vale of sorrow into a far better land of promise*. The words of Christ can lead us and guide us, just like the Liahona led and directed Nephi and his family to the promised land.

As Alma finishes explaining the power of this sacred record, he shares this important truth. "And the Lord God doth work *by means* to bring about his great and eternal purposes; and by very small means the Lord doth confound the wise and bringeth about the salvation of many souls" (Alma 37:7).

The means he was talking about is the Book of Mormon.

From the Book of Mormon, I learned that heaven was close when I was thirteen years old.

Through the incredible power found in the Book of Mormon, I stayed in the MTC when I wanted to go home. By this means, I learned the Lord could teach me a complex language when I thought all was hopeless in Japan. I learned to give freely of my substance and to forgive others. I have felt comforted by God on more occasions than I can count and have also had my share of chastisement.

My life has been filled with special experiences, and I have seen the Lord's hand in my life on many occasions. But the number one thing that has anchored me to the Savior and His gospel is the Book of Mormon—hands down.

We really can learn to hear the voice of the Lord as we diligently study the Book of Mormon every day. Our loving Father and Brother Jesus Christ yearn to communicate with us. They want to lead us. They want us to know they are real, through the power of the Holy Ghost.

"The way is prepared, and if we will look we may live forever" (Alma 37:46).

CHAPTER 3

*"And Elijah came unto all the people, and said,
How long halt ye between two opinions? if
the Lord be God, follow him…"*

1 Kings 18:21

E lijah was an Old Testament prophet (1 Kings 17-
19) who taught us some important lessons as he
traversed a terrible famine in the land. He was kept
alive at the beginning of the famine by ravens that
flew in and brought him food every day. I'm not
kidding. Birds brought him his meals. I don't know
if they chewed it up and spit it in his mouth the
way they do when feeding their babies. I hope not.
I like to imagine they just snatched up a rabbit and
dropped it at his feet, and he then cooked it up and
ate it. Literally feeding him chewed-up food makes me
want to barf a little, so I'm going to imagine the latter.

"Oh, thanks, dear raven, for this rabbit. You
saved the day again. You can go now." That's how
that scene went. Don't worry about it.

The Lord takes care of his people. Sometimes it's
not the way we suspect or think we want, i.e., Raven

Uber Eats. But the Lord takes care of those who put their trust in Him.

During the aforementioned famine, King Ahab, the king of Israel, encouraged the people to worship a God named Baal. King Ahab told the people that Baal would save the day and end the famine.

After a while, the people stop worshipping the God of their fathers and start worshiping this God, Baal. Because of this, God sent Elijah to King Ahab to show the people that they were mistaken. And take note—because this is what *God always does*. When the people are confused or heading down the wrong path, He sends His prophets to straighten things out.

Elijah invited all the people in town and the 450 priests of Baal up on a mountain to have a little showdown. God wanted the people to know who it was they should worship and who the real God was.

When all the people get there, Elijah asked them a simple question:

"How long halt ye between two opinions?"

He continues by saying, "if the Lord be God, follow him: but if Baal, then follow him" (1 Kings 18:21).

If I'm going to paint the scene here, I want to say that I bet there were a lot of good people there. The faithful Israelites who had followed Moses out of town and had walked through the Red Sea on dry ground were their ancestors. They were a people with a righteous history, but at the moment, they were confused. It's pretty easy to see how it happened. Some very important people had persuaded them to believe things that were just not true.

And we can't forget that they were in the middle of a famine. They were thirsty and hungry and had inadvertently let the voices of 450 priests, the king, and the king's household sway them away from their God. They had been deceived and were confused, so they were ready for some clarity.

Elijah then presented God's plan to the people and to the priests. He proposed that he and the priests of Baal burn sacrifices for the Lord upon an altar—build up the wood and prepare the animal sacrifice. But there was one caveat—they can't use any fire. They had to ask their respective gods to light their offerings.

The priests agreed, and the people watched. The priests of Baal went first and prepared their altar and started praying. "Light this fire! Oh, Baal, please light this up. Come on, pal, you can do it." They continued praying like this all morning. The scriptures even say that they jumped up on the altar and ranted around, begging for it to be lit.

When noon came around, it says that Elijah mocked them by saying, "Cry aloud: for he is a god; either he is talking, or he is pursuing, or he is in a journey, or peradventure he sleepeth, and must be awaked" (1 Kings 18:27). When they heard this, they started to lose their minds. They start cutting themselves and letting the blood run all over.

I like the Old Testament. It's full of wild stories and people who do crazy things—like these priests. I don't know why they thought that slicing themselves up while standing on the altar would get things moving, but that's what they did.

They did this all day, but it didn't work. No fire, just a broken altar, and apparently some of their own blood all over.

When night came, Elijah moved in to show whose gód was really in charge. He fixed the broken altar and had the people dig a trench around it. He asks them to fill the trench with water and dump the water over the wood and the offering three times. This must have taken some faith. These people didn't have a lot of water—they were still in a relentless drought. But they did it. And it was important because Elijah needed all who were there to know that it wasn't some trick. The place was soaked. If it were lit now, it would have to be by the power of God.

Elijah then prayed to the Lord:

> Lord God of Abraham, Isaac, and of Israel, let it be known this day that thou art God in Israel, and that I am thy servant, and that I have done all these things at thy word. Hear me, O Lord, hear me, that this people may know that thou art the Lord God, and that thou hast turned their heart back again (1 Kings 18:36).

I like that he mentions turning their hearts back to God. This is what he wanted. *This* was the true miracle he was seeking.

It then says that "the fire of the Lord fell, and consumed the burnt sacrifice, and the wood, and the stones, and the dust, and licked up the water that was in the trench. And when all the people saw it, they fell on their faces: and they said, The Lord, he is the God; the Lord, he is the God" (1 Kings 18:38-39).

Both miracles happened. The fire lit the sacrifice, and the people turned back to God. It was an incredible miracle.

You might be thinking, *That's great and all, but why is she telling us an Old Testament story when she is trying to teach us about the power of the Book of Mormon?*

For two reasons.

The first revolves around the question, "How long halt ye between two opinions?"

We live in an age where people are being deceived. People are letting the persuasions of men scream louder than the prophets or the whispering of the Holy Ghost. We are letting money, busyness, confusion, distraction, and temptation pull us away from the God we love. We are figuratively worshiping Baal, and I don't think we recognize it fully.

We need to decide right now, "if the Lord be God, follow Him."

The days of wishy-washy worship are passed. We need to secure our foundation, and the first step is to decide to let God prevail. We need to learn to hear His voice. We need the courage to follow the prophet's admonitions.

The second reason I wanted to share this story is that I am as confident as Elijah that *God will light your sacrifice*. As you dive in and make studying the Book of Mormon a daily priority, God will bless your efforts. Your heart will soften. You will begin to feel Christ's love. After a time, you too will come to know in powerful ways that "the Lord, He is the God."

I feel a little like Elijah must have felt right before the fire rained down. I'm so excited for you to see what God can do.

CHAPTER 4

"Don't worry about your clumsily expressed feelings. Just talk to your compassionate, understanding Father. You are His precious child whom He loves perfectly and wants to help. As you pray, recognize that Father in Heaven is near and He is listening."

Elder Richard G. Scott

"Anywhere in the world except Japan!" I yelled to a group of friends as I left their apartment to head to mine for the night. My mission call would probably come the next day, and we were all taking our final guesses. I had made it perfectly clear that I did not want to learn a foreign language, and I didn't want to eat raw fish. I don't know why I joked so much about going to Japan, but I guess it was because it was the most foreign place I could think of. No thank you!

What I really wanted was to serve at Temple Square or in Nauvoo; that's where they led tours. I could just imagine myself walking in front of a group of enthralled tourists. With a dramatic wave of my arm, I would say, "And over here, we have the Seagull Monument."

They would follow as I said, "We're walking. We're walking."

Everyone would be, oh, so amazed at all I knew and at how funny I was, and they'd all line up to be baptized after one of my tours. I don't even remember having a companion in those daydreams. Who needed one? I was articulate and knew the gospel. Piece. Of. Cake.

When I opened my mission call and read Kobe, Japan, my dreams of perfectly born testimony and praise and recognition for a job well done circled down the drain.

What the what?

For real?

How did this happen?

I now have my theories. I think the Lord proclaims over and over in the scriptures that He will have a humble people. We do not give direction to the Lord; we take it from Him. And I think at some point, He may have said, "Melanie, do it. Make fun of going to Japan just one more time. And you'll see..." Or maybe He just realized my propensity for never shutting my mouth and knew that if people were going to learn the gospel from me, they would need to be able to get a word in edgewise. Either way, there I sat, knowing that I was doomed to failure.

Before a missionary heads out to serve their mission, they go to a place called The Missionary Training Center (MTC). Here the missionaries learn more about the gospel and different ways to effectively teach it to strangers. If a missionary happens to be going to a foreign country, they spend an intense two months studying that new language every day. Missionaries also get opportunities to hear from inspiring church leaders and time to read and study on their own.

The MTC was really hard for me for a zillion reasons. The most blaring was the fact that I have really bad ADHD. Sitting in a classroom for ten hours a day was not the perfect fit for me. I struggled to learn the language. I couldn't concentrate, and I couldn't remember anything. It was as bad as I had imagined.

Adding to that, I was a night owl and hated the mornings. I loved going to the movies, dating, and playing all night long. Now it was strict bedtime at 10 p.m., and up at 6:00 a.m. I would stare at the ceiling for hours in my bed at night, trying to fall asleep and stagger out of bed, angry and tired every morning.

I'll have to admit I loved teaching the discussions, going to devotionals and firesides, and learning more about the gospel. My faith and testimony were strong, and I loved to share them. That was why I was on a mission. It was my thing. I loved everything that had to do with that—but in English, not in NIHONGO.

There was another advantage. We could eat cereal for breakfast, lunch, and dinner if we wanted to. They even had Captain Crunch. I was a poor college student who could rarely afford meat or cereal, so the MTC was a great place—at least for food. It tasted really good to me, and it was all you could eat, so we all chowed down. But it did cause a small problem: GAS. Yep, it made all of us pretty gassy. I don't know why exactly, but ten of us trapped in a tiny room all day led to some not-so-great moments.

One day, as we were studying and learning, and it was perfectly quiet, and I mean pin-drop quiet, my companion, um ... passed gas really loudly. I turned to her and burst out laughing. "Sister Christensen! Hahahaha!"

And do you know what she did? She kept working, barely looking up at me or anyone else. She didn't turn red or act like she had done it at all. And because I had made the huge outburst, it looked like I had done it.

"Claim it!" I demanded. "Claim it!" But Sister Christensen just looked at me like I was being ridiculous and went back to her work. The whole room thought it was me.

We went through the rest of the day and had a pretty normal day, I guess. I don't remember beating her in the hall after class as I should have. I don't remember anything more about it until that night. As we knelt by our beds to have companionship prayer, she said, "And thank you, Heavenly Father, for letting Melanie claim my fart, so I didn't have to." I busted up laughing, and then she did too, and we couldn't stop.

Our roommates were already in bed and told us to leave the room. We lay in the hallway outside the door and laughed until all the laughter tears dried up. We had forgotten to take our key, and by then, our roommates were fast asleep. We had to wake them to let us back in. I don't think they were our biggest fans that night.

If you just clutched your pearls and judged me for telling a story about farts, then I guess I'll give you a lesson you can use.

Sister Christensen talked to God like He was a real person. She was grateful that I had taken the fall for her, so she thanked Heavenly Father for it. The irreverence was on me because I busted out laughing, which made her laugh. But it was cool. I bet she still prays like that, and I bet her kids do too.

I hope you remember this story next week when you are thankful the baby barfed on your husband and not you. Please remember my sweet companion's prayer when you're glad the bishop didn't hear that word your six-year-old yelled at his brother for breaking his crayon during testimony meeting. Thank Heavenly Father tonight that the lady at the Swig window accidentally stayed open five minutes late when what you needed most was a Diet Coke© at the end of a very hard day.

Don't think Heavenly Father doesn't want to hear everything that you were grateful for today. He does. He loves you and wants to hear about *all* the things that make you happy. Don't make God out to be some guy who only cares about what you say from the pulpit during testimony meetings. You'll never approach that guy. God is your dad in heaven. He wants to hear from you, even your funny stories.

I want to clarify; I'm not saying to be irreverent. I'm not saying to be too casual in the way we speak to deity. What I am saying is that we have to believe that our Father in Heaven is a person who wants to be close to us. He wants to hear about our triumphs and our sorrows. He especially wants to hear about everything we are grateful for.

A man named Daniel Tyler was with the prophet Joseph Smith, in Kirtland, at a time when so many people had turned their backs on the prophet. Daniel describes an occasion when he was present as the prophet prayed.

> I had heard men and women pray ... from the most ignorant, both as to letters and intellect, to the most learned and eloquent, but never until then had I heard a man address his Maker as though He was present listening as a kind father would listen to the sorrows of a dutiful child. Joseph was at that time unlearned, but that prayer ... partook of the learning and eloquence of heaven. There was no ostentation, no raising of the voice as by enthusiasm, but a plain conversational tone, as a man would address a present friend. It appeared to me as though, in case the veil were taken away, I could see the Lord standing facing His humblest of servants I had ever seen.[8]

Joseph spoke to God as he would speak to a friend. This was because God had become his friend, and he knew Him intimately.

Let God be your friend, the one standing just beyond the veil, waiting to hear about *all* of your life.

Elder Richard G. Scott said:

> Don't worry about your clumsily expressed feelings. Just talk to your compassionate, un-

derstanding Father. You are His precious child whom He loves perfectly and wants to help. As you pray, recognize that Father in Heaven is near and He is listening.[9]

CHAPTER 5

"Within the [Book of Mormon's] pages, you will discover the infinite love and incomprehensible grace of God. As you strive to follow the teachings you find there, your joy will expand, your understanding will increase, and the answers you seek to the many challenges mortality presents will be opened to you. As you look to the book, you look to the Lord."

Elder Gary E. Stevenson

Although the MTC had good food and I'd had some funny experiences, I was still really struggling. I didn't love being trapped in a classroom all day, and I didn't love learning the Japanese language. The waking and sleeping times were the opposite of mine, and I missed the people outside of the MTC. And don't forget the gas problem.

Everything came to a head one night. I no longer remember the cause. Maybe it was a culmination of a hard day or days, or perhaps it was one specific thing that set me off, but the point is I hit my breaking point.

I went into our room, pulled my suitcase out from under my bed, and started packing up my things. I was done. This was not for me. I had wanted to serve a mission for years, but not like this. I just couldn't do it. It was just too hard.

As I continued to throw things in my suitcase, my companion looked on, maybe not knowing if I was serious or not. Oh, I was! As I picked up my set of scriptures to throw it in the suitcase, I thought, *Ok, Heavenly Father. You have one chance to keep me here. Let's see what You have to say.*

I knew the Lord could speak to me through the scriptures, as it had happened a few times before. And I knew that although I was acting like a spoiled baby, I still wanted direction in my life. But I thought the direction would be to leave. I really did, as I wasn't cutting it.

I opened the door and sat down on the little orange chair outside our room. I opened right to where I was because I knew this always worked for me. There was no need to look up "missionary temper tantrum" in the topical guide. When I opened to my bookmark, I found that I was in the war chapters of Alma.

Haha, Heavenly Father. I'm going home! What can you teach me in the war chapters?

I started to read in Alma 56. Here, the Nephite army was being led by a man named Antipus. It said that Antipus and his army were "depressed in body as well as in spirit, ... and had suffered great afflictions of every kind" (Alma 56:16). I could relate! Going to bed at 10 p.m. was almost as bad as fighting in a long, drawn-out, gruesome war, right? And don't forget sitting in a classroom all day! I had it rough. Ok, maybe not compared to Antipus and his men, but I was depressed in spirit, and I was tired of my circumstances.

Many of Antipus's men had been taken prisoner, and many more had been killed. They were desperately struggling to fortify their city but were discouraged. At this point, Helaman shows up with 2,000 young men to help. Their parents had made an oath never to take up weapons of war again. But because these boys hadn't made the oath, they decided to go help out. What a relief the sight of those boys were to Antipus and his army.

To make a long story short, Antipus and Helaman hatched a plan. They decided that Helaman and his army of boys would only act as a decoy to lure the Lamanites out of their stronghold. Once out, Antipus and his army could then fight them on common ground. These boys weren't going to have to fight; they just had to run.

Helaman's army marched past the Lamanite city, and just as planned, the Lamanite army came out after them. The Lamanites chased after Helaman's boys. The boys began to book it. This continued for two days. Helaman and his boys were just running. That was the plan anyway—they weren't prepared to fight, and they wouldn't be strong enough to win on their own.

On the morning of the third day, they started running again, but the Lamanite army didn't follow them. The Lamanites had turned to fight Antipus, so Antipus undoubtedly needed help.

Worried, Helaman asked these young boys, "... what say ye, my sons, will ye go against them to battle?" (Alma 56:44).

Helaman recounted what happened in a letter to Captain Moroni. Helaman explained:

And now I say unto you, my beloved brother Moroni, that never had I seen so great courage, nay, not amongst all the Nephites. For as I had ever called them my sons (for they were all of them very young) even so they said unto me: Father, behold our God is with us, and he will not suffer that we should fall; then let us go forth; we would not slay our brethren if they would let us alone; therefore let us go, lest they should overpower the army of Antipus. Now they never had fought, yet they did not fear death; and they did think more upon the liberty of their fathers than they did upon their lives; yea, they had been taught by their mothers, that if they did not doubt, God would deliver them. And they rehearsed unto me the words of their mothers, saying: We do not doubt our mothers knew it (Alma 56:45-48).

When I read the words, "they did think more upon the liberty of their fathers than they did upon their lives ...," I stopped. The Red Sea parted right there in the hallway, and the Lord taught me what I needed to know.

All of a sudden, I was one of those boys. I was running. Running from learning Japanese and running back to the world I had left behind. I was running from too many rules and not enough me time. I knew I had to stop running and make a choice. I needed to think more about those sweet Japanese people who were waiting to hear the gospel than I did about my own personal wants. I needed to have faith and courage like those boys. They had never fought, and yet they trusted God. I had never been to Japan and was pretty sure that I would never learn the language. But like these boys, I too had been taught by righteous parents that if I did not doubt, God would deliver me.

With a heart full of the Spirit and some newly found humility, I closed my scriptures and went back into our room. I put my suitcase away and decided to stay. My Liahona had led the way once again.

Jesus Christ and our Heavenly Father had the ability to get a powerful message to me in the war chapters of Alma. I heard the words of Christ whisper in my ear, through the power of the Holy Ghost, that I should stay in the MTC and that I should go to Japan. That evening, sitting on that sticky, orange vinyl chair outside my room, with my head leaning against that brick wall, I again felt so much love from heaven.

Yeah, I was being a baby. Yes, my challenges were not that big. But instead of the Lord telling me what a brat I was, He placed in front of me the image of those Japanese people waiting for the blessings of the gospel. Christ gave me a pep talk in the form of 2,000 brave boys marching to battle and trusting in the Lord. I love those righteous boys, and that night I wanted to be like them. I hope someday I get to hug those boys and thank them for their courage and faith.

And my gosh, how I love those mammas! I'm sure none of them had any clue that far, far in the future, their righteous testimonies and the words they taught their boys would change the course of my life. I want to be like them. I want my kids to say with confidence, "We do not doubt our mother knew it."

Elder Gary E Stevenson once said:

> Within the [Book of Mormon's] pages, you will discover the infinite love and incomprehensible grace of God. As you strive to follow the teachings you find there, your joy will expand, your understanding will increase, and the answers you seek to the many challenges mortality presents will be opened to you. As you look to the book, you look to the Lord.[10]

By turning to the Book of Mormon, I opened communication with my Savior. I turned to Him, and He turned to me. How often Christ admonishes us, "...ask, and ye shall receive; knock, and it shall be opened unto you; for he that asketh, receiveth; and unto him that knocketh, it shall be opened" (3 Nephi 27:29).

CHAPTER 6

"Nevertheless they did fast and pray oft, and did wax stronger and stronger in their humility, and firmer and firmer in the faith of Christ, unto the filling their souls with joy and consolation, yea, even to the purifying and the sanctification of their hearts, which sanctification cometh because of their yielding their hearts unto God."

Helaman 3:35

When I finally got to Japan two months later, I was first assigned to serve in Kyoto. When you think of Japan, Kyoto is what you imagine—prominent temples and bright orange arches, canals, and quaint little streets. Bent, little old ladies pushed their walkers through town. Small restaurants are adorned with large black, white, and red vertical banners, beckoning hungry patrons. We would ride our bikes daily past tight cemeteries crammed full of headstones and treats left there by mourning family members. School kids in uniforms with matching hats and backpacks filled the streets.

If you want to experience everything you see in a travel brochure for Japan, plunk yourself down in Kyoto—they even have a GOLD temple there. And to top it off, I happened to get there in March, right as the cherry blossoms were in full bloom. I felt as if I had walked onto a beautiful movie set. Heavenly Father had spared no detail in welcoming me to Japan. Maybe this wasn't going to be so bad after all.

My trainer, Sister Wilder, was precisely as the mission president had said. "She's so great. I think you two will hit it off." And he was right. She was a hoot. She was fun and good and beautiful and smart and a hard worker. She wore Doc Martins under her skirts and rode her bike like a champ. Did I mention we were on bikes, with helmets, in dresses? Yikes.

With this magnificent start, I began to serve—and then real life set in, quickly. I was a terrible bike rider. I didn't like the food. And I quickly realized I had basically only eaten sugar my whole life and was now in full-fledged sugar withdrawal. Oh, and as I figured, I couldn't speak or understand anything anyone said.

But all of this was ok because Sister Wilder was patient, good, kind, and amazing. She was just what I needed. And she worked hard.

In Japan, you don't do a lot of door-knocking. It just doesn't work and is not effective. People had these little boxes outside their door that contained a speaker. You would click on the speaker and explain why you are there—like the equivalent of a RING doorbell, minus the video. They don't get to see the light in your eyes or your beautiful faces. They just hear your voice.

We would explain who we were, and they would always reply, "Kekko desu," which meant, "We are ok." We called them kekko boxes, and thus, we didn't knock on doors much to find investigators.

The way we did find people to teach was through teaching free English classes at the church. Everyone wanted to learn English, and free is a universally liked concept.

We distributed flyers about our English classes when we needed to find people to teach; areas that had big English classes had large teaching pools. It was effective.

When new students would come to the church, we would give them a little interview before class. We explained that we were missionaries and were in Japan to teach people about Jesus Christ. We said that we were teaching English as a service and that there was no obligation to convert or hear more about the gospel. This was true. We weren't trying to trick them, and we wanted them to know our motives from the start. We then told them that we would share a message or do an activity related to the gospel after English class, and they were welcome to stay if they wanted. It was a great way to prose-lyte. I loved it. I wanted to be a speech therapist, so drilling the Japanese on their pronunciation was a blast.

One night in English class, I was my usual, crazy self. I was laughing and playing around—we were having a great time. After class, one of our investiga-tors pulled me aside and said, "Every kind of person needs to hear about the gospel—that's why you are here."

Her words came back to me the other day as I pretended to be Pharoah's wife on my podcast. I was talking with a crazy accent and complaining about the noisy frogs. I thought, *What in the world am I even doing? I have gone off the rails!* And then that sweet Japanese girl's words came to my mind.

It's ok. All of us learn differently. Like me, some just need a little laughter mixed with feeling the Spirit. I hope it doesn't offend you. Heavenly Father gave me this personality for a reason. He knows some just need to hear the gospel from a friend—someone they can relate to, someone who is a lot like them.

And that's me. Because I am just like you. And that's the coolest part of what I'm about to teach you. God doesn't expect us to be perfect in order to speak to us, lead us, and guide us. He just wants us to humbly turn to Him on a regular basis. In fact, "The word initiates and increases our faith in Christ and fuels within us a desire to become more like the Savior—that is, to repent and walk on the covenant path."[11] It's a cool byproduct. When we come to Him in our not-so-perfect natures, and as we return again and again to His word, we develop the desire to become better. We don't have to stay jerks forever. Yay!

I was in Kyoto for most of my mission. I served there for eight months. I witnessed my first fireflies, had my first bike wreck, and ate my first octopus and intestines—all in Kyoto. It was there that I taught the most people, saw my only baptisms, and served with my favorite people.

Looking back, the Lord knew what He was doing when He sent me all the way across the sea to teach people about the gospel in such a foreign way. It was there that Heavenly Father needed to teach me the one lesson that would change my life and the life of thousands of others across the world.

But why did He have to send me to Japan to learn this lesson? There were plenty of missions in the United States where mission presidents taught with inspiration and passion about the power of the Book of Mormon. I had loved the gospel since I was a small child and loved talking about it. Why send me somewhere where my tongue would basically stay tied the whole time? Why send me somewhere where I could share so little of what was in my heart? Why Japan?

There is a scripture in the Book of Mormon that reveals the answer.

Nevertheless they did fast and pray oft, and did wax stronger and stronger in their humility, and firmer and firmer in the faith of Christ, unto the filling their souls with joy and consolation, yea, even to the purifying and the sanctification of their hearts, which sanctification cometh because of their yielding their hearts unto God (Helaman 3:35).

This is why I had to go to Japan.

Japan took the pride out of me. It was there that I learned how to yield my heart to God.

I thought I was a pretty big deal back then. I thought I knew the gospel well and would be an amazing missionary. I had a lot of faith in *myself* and a lot of love for my Father in heaven. But God had to take away my power of speech so I would finally learn to listen. He had to take me to the depths of humility in order to learn how to hear His voice. I couldn't serve a full-time mission in Japan on my own. I needed the power of God in my life to lead and direct me. I needed to learn how God could speak to me, and I needed to be reminded there—so far away from all the people that I loved and counted on—that I was not alone. In that first area, I learned so many vital lessons that brought me closer to the Savior and His gospel.

And it was there that our mission president taught us a "new way" to study the Book of Mormon.

CHAPTER 7

The Plan

A few months into my mission, our mission president told us at a zone conference that he had been praying about us and what we could do to become better missionaries. He said that he was inspired to give us a five-step method for studying the scriptures. There was nothing in this plan that was particularly new or earth-shattering. There were conference talks and primary songs that include many of these steps. "Search. Ponder and Pray" is the actual name of a primary song.[12] We have heard these things all our lives, but there is something about these particular steps, in this particular order, that really helps revelation freely flow.

He taught us five steps that he felt the Lord wanted us to learn in order to receive revelation. I began studying the Book of Mormon like this in 1994 in Kyoto, Japan, and have continued to do this for the last twenty-eight years. I believe that this one simple habit, repeated over and over again, is what saved me from so many of the spiritual traps and roadblocks that caused so many of my friends and family to lose their faith.

Reading the Book of Mormon, like this, every day saved my spiritual life.

Here is the plan:

1. Pray

Express gratitude. Be thankful for everything you can think of.

Repent. Clear the air between you and the Lord. Be humble.

Ask to gain knowledge and inspiration. If you have a specific question or worry, ask to get clarification about it.

2. Read

Not necessarily a chapter a day. Smaller portions. Learn to cross-reference.

3. Ponder

What does this have to do with me, my family, etc.? Why was this saved for my day? How can I apply what I'm reading to my life?

4. Write

Write down the scriptures that touch you and your feelings about them.

5. Pray again

Ask for help and guidance to apply the things you learned.

Thank Heavenly Father again for the rare opportunity you have to have the Book of Mormon.

CHAPTER 8

"The Lord has a way of pouring pure intelligence into our minds to prompt us, to guide us, to teach us, to warn us. You can know the things you need to know instantly! Learn to receive inspiration."[13]

Elder Boyd K. Packer

T he key to this method is to set aside a *block of time* every day that you are going to read. Throw out the idea of a chapter a day. Some days you may only end up reading one verse! It's also great if you can pick the same time every day to do it. Wake up thirty minutes before your family wakes up. Promise to turn in thirty minutes before you actually want to go to sleep. Say, "I will study the first twenty minutes of my lunch break every day." Make a plan, and then commit it to your Father in Heaven. "Heavenly Father, please help me to read every day. Please help me to find answers and to be able to hear Your voice." I like asking Him to bless the things that are important to me. He wants us to succeed as much as we want to. Ask Heavenly Father for His help to make this study a daily routine. Ask for patience and perseverance as you begin to study in this way.

I feel best when I do this first thing in the morning. Communicating with God first thing sets the tone for my day. When I fill my heart with God's words in the morning, my days seem to go smoother. I'm softer, and it's easier to tackle the hard. I feel I'm more patient, more kind. Maybe that's the reason seminary is almost always early in the morning, before high school starts. The Lord knows how hard school is for teenagers. He knows high school can give kids trying to follow Jesus quite a beating. Filling them with goodness, even if it is through osmosis because they are half asleep, has the same desired benefits.

Turning to Him first thing each day is like knocking on His door and waiting for Him to open it. When He does, I see myself saying, "Hi, I'm just wondering if You'll be a part of my day today?"

Do you know what I always imagine Him saying?

"Sure, I was hoping you would ask."

It's also so important to turn to the Book of Mormon *every day*. President Thomas S. Monson pleaded, "I implore each of us to prayerfully study and ponder the Book of Mormon each day. As we do so, we will be in a position to hear the voice of the Spirit, to resist temptation, to overcome doubt and fear, and to receive heaven's help in our lives."[14]

Problem is, even if we believe this is true, so many things compete for our time and attention on a daily basis.

This Design Home game can't play itself!

Hold, please! I need to scroll through social media for hours so that I can see all the perfect kitchens with fresh hydrangeas on the counters. There's that ad for that Noom app again. Maybe I should start a diet. Did I just eat another donut? What's wrong with me?! Look at my kitchen! Where are the flowers? I can smell that dirty sponge from here. Are those last night's dishes still in the sink? Ooh, speaking of sinks, I need to go look for those cute pink gloves for washing dishes on Amazon. Who posted those the other day?

Hours and countless rabbit holes later, I have not read my scriptures or done much of anything.

See! Distraction is one of Satan's greatest tools.

I recently found Sudoku. My jerk friend Kelly gave me a book for Christmas and some pencils. I can get stuck there for hours. The other day I was playing Sudoku in my book while watching *Jeopardy*. My fifteen-year-old walked in and laughed and asked, "Are you old?" I looked down at my book and up at the TV.

"I guess I am."

Dang it!

Wait. Why am I telling you all *my* time-wasters? You've got your own.

All I'm saying is that it's easy to let things edge out that time we have with the scriptures every day, even good things. In a talk called, "Good, Better, Best," President Dallin H Oaks said:

> Just because something is good is not a sufficient reason for doing it. The number of good things we can do far exceeds the time available to accomplish them. Some things are better

than good, and these are the things that should command priority attention in our lives.[15]

Certainly, taking time to study and ponder the Book of Mormon every day belongs in the BEST category.

Reading the Book of Mormon every day is more important than studying any other book. *Come Follow Me*, as great as it is, wasn't made to trump our study of the Book of Mormon.

At the very beginning of the *Come Follow Me* manual, it says, "Come, Follow Me—For Individuals and Families is not meant to replace or compete with other good things you are doing. Follow the Spirit's guidance to determine how to approach your own study of the word of God."[16]

If you want to follow the guidance in that manual, ask God to help you determine how much time you need to spend in the scriptures and where. God knows the power of the Book of Mormon and what it will do to help you develop a relationship with Him and His Son.

Recently President Nelson drove this point home: "My brothers and sisters, I plead with you to make time for the Lord! Make your own spiritual foundation firm and able to stand the test of time by doing those things that allow the Holy Ghost to be with you *always*."[17]

President Harold B. Lee gave us another good reason to make daily study a priority. He said, "If we're not reading the scriptures daily, our testimonies are growing thinner [and] our spirituality isn't increasing in depth."[18]

And if the testimonies of two prophets aren't enough, maybe stick these words in your mind. "If you don't read the scriptures every day, you will probably slip and fall on the ice outside, choke on a chicken bone, and your last screaming rant including any swears will be posted to your Facebook page for the world to see, forever." Someone really important said that.

CHAPTER 9

*"There is nothing more helpful than prayer
to open our understanding of the scriptures.
Through prayer we can attune our minds to seek
the answers to our searchings. The Lord said:
"Ask, and it shall be given you; seek, and ye
shall find; knock, and it shall be opened unto
you" (Luke 11:9). Herein is Christ's reassurance
that if we will ask, seek, and knock, the Holy
Spirit will guide our understanding if we are
ready and eager to receive."[19]*

President Howard W. Hunter

Step 1.0 Pray

In Japan, we slept on the floor on little mats called
futons. In America, we usually put these small
mattresses on nice wood or metal frames, which are
off the ground. They can work as both a couch and
a bed. But in Japan, they are thin, little things that
we folded up in the morning and put in the closet. Space was limited, so who would ever think to

put those on a wood frame that turns into a little couch we could use all day? Who would want to sit on a sofa like a sucker when you can kneel on the floor on a scratchy mat all day in a dress? I think the Japanese people may have invented the word futon, but we Americans have made them much more comfortable and functional.

In Japan, when we prayed at night, we were technically on our knees. But I had gotten in a bad habit of putting my head down on my pillow, my rear end sort of in the air as I prayed. For those yoga enthusiasts, it was like *downward dog*, but on my knees.

When we studied at our little tables on the floor, we were either sitting cross-legged under them or kneeling flat. Although we were constantly kneeling, it wasn't prayer style, like when you kneel in front of your bed and bow your head. At least it didn't feel like that to me. Thus, I had become super casual with my prayers.

In my second area, a little town called Kakagowa, our apartment had little desks with actual chairs. While reading the Book of Mormon one morning, I read something about prayer. I remember feeling a little chastised by the Lord that I had not been very reverent and should get down on my knees to pray.

That's it.

Isn't that a great story?

I don't remember anything else about that experience or that day, but it is an experience that often comes to my mind. Sometimes I think about it as I pray in the shower or in my car. Perhaps it pops up when I'm praying in bed, too tired to get out and on my knees. It has flashed back to my mind when

I start to pray in my head about something, and my mind wanders all over the place. Later, when I get done and move on to the next activity, I ask myself, "Did I finish that prayer?"

Maybe you just judged me. Not finishing a prayer? "Well, I never!"

I don't know if this is other people's reality or not. Honestly, maybe everyone is sure they end every prayer, every time. If so, I'm very embarrassed I've just admitted this fact. My ADHD causes me to flit between activities and thoughts so fast it's almost comical.

If you took a peek into my brain, most days, it looks like a bunch of ping-pong balls that someone just knocked off a high shelf, and they are just bouncing all over the place.

Speaking of thoughts bouncing all over—here's my point. I remember getting down on my knees that day in Japan and giving a very purposeful prayer. When I have been most eager for an answer or most in need of the Spirit, I hit my knees *hard*. I begged the Lord, out loud, for what I needed. Praying out loud rather than in my head is crucial for me. It's like fasting. I'm telling the Lord I'm serious.

We are told in the Book of Mormon to pray in our closets and fields. We are told to have our hearts constantly drawn out in prayer; this I do. Heavenly Father has become a friend that I chat with a lot during my day. These types of prayers are necessary too.

But there is something very sweet about getting on your knees, alone, and praying aloud. If you're a mother of young children, this may have to happen in the closet or the bathroom. When you put the steps from this book into practice for the first time, maybe make your prayer a kneeling prayer. Show God you are serious. Show Him you want to know He is real. Kneeling shows humility. Kneeling shows reverence. Praying out loud when you are alone is powerful.

About a year after my first husband and I were married, we went to live with my ninety-three-year-old grandma. She was cool, fun, and sassy. We loved our time with her. She kept Moon-Pies®, Star Crunch®, and Oatmeal Cream Pies® in her dishwasher. One lady living alone doesn't make enough dishes to facilitate a dishwasher. The space became the biggest Grandma cookie jar of all. She also kept Hershey's® bars in her crisper in the fridge and hid money in her china cabinet.

When we first moved in with her, she hadn't gone to church in a while because she couldn't hear well, which made her uncomfortable. While living with her, Christmas happened to fall on a Sunday or very near to it. She decided that she wanted to go to church that day. I have a picture somewhere of her in her pretty blue dress with a crocheted corsage pinned to it. We all went to church, and everyone was happy to see her. Because she couldn't hear well, she sang loud and a little off tempo, but it was great to have her with us. Everyone loved my grandma. She was just so much fun. It seemed like everyone wanted to say hi.

When we got home, she said, "Well, I'm not going to do that again!"

I was shocked. I thought it had been a great meeting.

"Grandma, why don't you want to go to church again?"

She laughed and said, "Not that."

"I wore this bra the whole time, and not one person came up to me and said, 'Thanks for wearing a bra today.'"

I almost fell to the ground laughing. She was a kick. I miss her a lot.

How did I get from praying on my knees to begrudgingly wearing bras to church? Oh ya, living with my almost deaf ninety-three-year-old grandma taught me some special lessons about prayer. Every night, she would kneel beside her bed and pray out loud. She took her hearing aids out before she went to sleep, so I don't think she realized how loud she was talking. Our bedroom was right next to hers, so we often heard her pray.

She would pray so specifically for everyone in the family. She would pray that my husband would do well on his test, or that I would have enough energy to continue teaching the kids with special needs at my school while almost ready to deliver my first baby. She would pray for my cousins that lived out of state and for my Uncle Tom and his wife. She would pray for my mom and her sister and my siblings and so many people. She would ask for good things to happen to all of us. She spent so much time thanking Him for all her blessings.

The only thing I ever remember hearing her ask for herself was at the end of the prayer. She would often say, "Please help me not to fall tomorrow." Her prayers were special. I'm so grateful for the year I spent living with her. What a blessing that was in my life.

Elder Richard G. Scott said:

> It matters not our circumstance, be we humble or arrogant, poor or rich, free or enslaved, learned or ignorant, loved or forsaken, we can address Him. We need no appointment. Our supplication can be brief or can occupy all the time needed. It can be an extended expression of love and gratitude or an urgent plea for help. He has created numberless cosmos and populated them with worlds, yet you and I can talk with Him personally, and He will ever answer.[20]

I love how Elder Scott talked about the fact that He who created the cosmos is waiting to hear from us. When my first husband, our daughter, and I lived in Virginia, I met a woman named Cheryl. I spoke to her after the first day that she came to church as an investigator. She was standing there, sobbing. I asked her what was wrong and she said, "I have never felt this amount of love before. It's overwhelming. I'm just not used to it." A little over a year later, I had the beautiful opportunity to be her escort as she went through the temple for the first time. When we were leaving the Washington D.C. temple, she turned to me and said, "I can't believe it. It's so amazing. I have a personal relationship with the Creator of the universe."

We do! We need to remember this as we pray. It's such a special thing.

A listener of my podcast wrote to me once, saying that her mom was always a great example of sincerely praying. She and her siblings would find their mom kneeling beside her bed, praying multiple times a day. She said that sometimes her mom would pray for so long that she or her siblings would go in and kneel beside her or shimmy up under her arms as she continued to pray. This listener said her mom would lift her arm and scratch their backs or hug them as she continued to pray. I wish I could go back in time and let my children see me on my knees more.

I wish I had spent more time on my knees in the middle of the day. I wish that when things were hard or some aspect of being a mother to five young children had gotten the best of me, I would have hit my knees more often. What I wouldn't give to have one of my adult or teenage children be tiny again for a day, nuzzle up beside me, and wait for me to finish talking to the Lord. You young parents, you still have the chance. Teach them the power of prayer by being on your knees a lot. It's a big deal.

Man, this book would be six pages long if I just got to the point! But instead, you will follow all of these meanderings through my mind for hundreds of pages.

I don't even feel bad. I love talking about good people who have taught me good things. If you thought that I would get straight to the point and stay focused even once in this book, you haven't listened to my podcast. This is who I am.

Sorry, not sorry.

There is a great scripture in the Doctrine and Covenants that I really like. Christ says, "...I say unto you, my friends, I leave these sayings with you to ponder in your hearts, with this commandment which I give unto you, that ye shall call upon me while I am near—Draw near unto me and I will draw near unto you;" (Doctrine and Covenants 88: 62-63).

I like the phrase, "Call upon me while I am near." I think we bring the Lord near when we open the scriptures. I like to imagine that I'm physically bringing the Savior near to me as I purposefully pray and then turn to my scriptures. When Jesus says, "Call upon me while I'm near," grab your scriptures and start praying. He then promises us that He will draw near to us. It's such a fun process. I love it.

Elder Scott said:

We talk to God through prayer. He most often communicates back to us through His written word. To know what the voice of the Divine sounds and feels like, read His words, study the scriptures, and ponder them. Make them an integral part of everyday life.[21]

CHAPTER 10

*"And one of them, when he saw that he was
healed, turned back, and with a loud voice
glorified God, And fell down on his face
at his feet, giving him thanks: and he was
a Samaritan. And Jesus answering said, "Were
there not ten cleansed? but where are the nine?"*

Luke 17:15-17

Step 1.1 Be Grateful

The first thing we were taught to do in this
prayer was *express gratitude*. Thank Heavenly
Father for the blessing of having the Book of Mormon in your life. Really. So many people have yet to
find it, but you have it. Somehow, out of billions of
people on earth, you have been blessed to have this
special testament of Jesus Christ in your possession.
What a blessing. Be thankful for the missionaries
who found you or found your parents or however
you came to own a copy or to be a member of this
church.

Jump from there. Thank God for your house or your family, or even your medication. After suffering a few days with a bad UTI, I remember that I prayed such a grateful prayer for antibiotics. Be thankful for music, Sunday naps, and your friend or cat. Gratitude does something special to our souls.

I'm reminded of the story of the ten lepers that Jesus healed. They came to Him begging to be healed from this awful ailment that had plagued them for so long. He told them to go and show themselves to the priest, and they would be healed.

I don't know how far away the priest was. They may have had to walk quite some distance. But they went there, and they were completely healed, all ten of them. But the story doesn't end there. This wasn't just a story about another of Christ's miracles or the power of our faith to be healed. Jesus had another important lesson to teach us. The scene ended like this:

> And one of them, when he saw that he was healed, turned back, and with a loud voice glorified God, And fell down on his face at his feet, giving him thanks: and he was a Samaritan. And Jesus answering said, "Were there not ten cleansed? but where are the nine?" (Luke 17:15-17).

Why did Jesus add this part to the story?

He added it because gratitude is important to Jesus and our Heavenly Father. If you don't believe me, let me share a little jingle I learned while volunteering in my daughter's first-grade class. It went like this, "An-to-nyms are op-po-sites, an-to-nyms are op-po-sites." What is the opposite of thanking God for our blessings? What's the antonym of gratitude? This is an easy one; it's ingratitude. In the Doctrine and Covenants 59:21, it says, "And in nothing doth man offend God, or against none is his wrath kindled, save those who confess not his hand in all things, and obey not his commandments." Yikes.

Did you hear what God cares about most? In case you missed it, it's gratitude and keeping the commandments. Please don't freak out about the kindling wrath stuff right now. If you haven't been very grateful lately, who cares? Repent. Then start being more grateful. Once you start being grateful, you find more and more stuff to be grateful for. It's fun.

I have a few people in my life I give gifts to every year. One of these people often says something like, "Thanks. Do you have the receipt?" And the other person, my mother, says, "OH MY GOSH! This is the loveliest washcloth I've ever seen. I will use it every day. It's such a great color, and have you felt it? It's soooo soft!" I call it the "Mom gush." She's really good at it, and she's sincere. I love giving her things.

Which of these two people would you rather give a gift to?

I imagine Heavenly Father feels a little bit the same way. When we sit down and pray and thank Heavenly Father for all the ways we have seen His hand in our lives, it makes Him happy. And I think the more we acknowledge Him, the more He wants to give us. I'm serious. I think Heavenly Father knows that I see His hand in my life. I look for it. I see the ways He blesses me, and not only do I see it, I tell others about it. I'm a gusher by blood, and God loves gushing. I can feel it.

Like my example, I think He gets ready to send more blessings my way because it's fun for Him to give to the grateful.

"I, the Lord, am willing, if any among you desire to ride upon horses, or upon mules, or in chariots, he shall receive this blessing, if he receive it from the hand of the Lord, with a thankful heart in all things" (Doctrine and Covenants 62:7).

See? Start gushing and see what happens.

But you've got to be sincere about it. Fake gush doesn't work.

The 2020 Youth Theme Song, "Go and Do," includes such inspired counsel. I think about it all the time. This one line is a sermon in and of itself. "When I feel overcome, and all my strength is gone, I think of all the ways he's blessed me."[22]

He may be blessing you more than you even realize. Taking the time to look for and be grateful for God's blessings often brings more experiences to your remembrance.

Elder Rasband reminds us, "Many of you have witnessed miracles, more than you realize. They may seem small in comparison to Jesus raising the dead. But the magnitude does not distinguish a miracle, only that it came from God."[23]

Having gratitude and being thankful can give us strength. It pulls us out of sadness and brings back joy. That's why it is so important to be grateful before you start reading The Book of Mormon. Gratitude prepares us to feel God's love in more abundance. And when we sit down to read the scriptures, that's what we should be hoping to find and feel— God's overwhelming love for us.

If you can't think of anything to be thankful for because things are really hard right now, that's ok. Life gets complicated, and sometimes coming before God, gratefully, is difficult. So just say you're thankful to have the Book of Mormon.

It's enough for now.

CHAPTER 11

"We can feel godly sorrow for our actions and, at the same time, feel the joy of having the Savior's help. The fact that we can repent is the good news of the gospel! Guilt can be 'swept away.' We can be filled with joy, receive a remission of our sins, and have 'peace of conscience.' We can be freed from feelings of despair and the bondage of sin. We can be filled with the marvelous light of God and be 'pained no more.' Repentance is not only possible but also joyful because of our Savior."

Elder Dale G. Renlund

Step 1.2 Repent

What I have learned from a lifetime of feasting on the words of Christ is this: Christ loves us so much. He loves it when we repent. We read in the Doctrine and Covenants, Section 18:11-13:

For, behold, the Lord your Redeemer suffered death in the flesh; wherefore he suffered the pain of all men, that all men might repent and come unto him. And he hath arisen again from the dead, that he might bring all men unto him, on conditions of repentance. And how great is his joy in the soul that repenteth!

We need to think about this when we repent. We need to think of the beautiful gift He gave to all of us because He loves us so much. We need to think of the joy that Heavenly Father and Jesus Christ feel as we turn to them and repent.

I really like a researcher named Brené Brown. She commonly talks about shame. She made a clarification that stuck with me. She talked about the difference between shame and guilt. Basically, guilt is 'I *did* that,' shame is 'I *am* that.'

The more I read and learn, I realize that shame doesn't come from God. You are never bad; you only *did* something bad. It's so important to keep this clear in your mind. God never uses shame.

Our Heavenly Father and His son, Jesus Christ, find joy when we acknowledge our mistakes and move forward. The pain for what we have done wrong, the guilt that motivates us to move forward and take care of our actions, comes from our Father in Heaven. But when we confess those sins and begin to forsake them, that guilt should begin to dissipate. No more guilt, and indeed no shame. Sure, there will be remorse and perhaps some embarrassment, but that motivating guilt should leave and be replaced with love.

I want to say something about embarrassment because I used that word. Our embarrassment over our sins sometimes hinders us from discussing more significant sins with the proper priesthood authority. I had a funny experience the other day that correlates, I promise.

I was at the gastroenterologist because of some bowel issues I was having and because I needed to schedule a colonoscopy. My dad died of colon cancer when he was forty-eight, and I was then forty-nine, and it had been too many years since my last colonoscopy. We were chatting about stuff that I don't usually chat with people about. As I began to tell the doctor some of my maladies, I stopped and said, "This is embarrassing." He looked at me and said, "Maybe for you, but it's not embarrassing for me. It's my job. I talk about this stuff all the time."

I think bishops probably feel this way. The Lord definitely does.

I imagine the Lord saying, like that doctor, "Do you think I haven't heard this one? Don't be embarrassed. I'm just glad you're here. Let's get this over with so you can move on and find peace and feel all My love again."

Remember Alma, when he told the story about when the angel came and said to him that he needed to knock off what he was doing? He said he was miserable thinking of everything he had done wrong. But then he remembered something his dad had said about this man named Jesus Christ.

In his words, he said, "And now, behold, when I thought this, I could remember my pains no more; yea, I was harrowed up by the memory of my sins no more. And oh, what joy, and what marvelous light I did behold; yea, my soul was filled with joy as exceeding as was my pain!" (Alma 36:19).

I can quote scriptures all day and repeatedly teach you the principle of repentance, but I know I don't need to. Regarding repentance, it sufficeth me to say, all I find is joy.

Elder Dale G. Renlund said:

> We can feel godly sorrow for our actions and, at the same time, feel the joy of having the Savior's help. The fact that we can repent is the good news of the gospel! Guilt can be "swept away." We can be filled with joy, receive a remission of our sins, and have "peace of conscience." We can be freed from feelings of despair and the bondage of sin. We can be filled with the marvelous light of God and be "pained no more." Repentance is not only possible but also joyful because of our Savior.[24]

I keep thinking about my friend's words to her daughter when she was repenting for looking at pornography. She told her, "You are *not less than* because you sinned, but *more than* because you repented. You are *more than* because you conquered Satan. You are *more than* because you are brave and confessed and don't want to do it anymore."

Her mom, having that attitude about it, took away the stigma. Soon after, her ward young women had a night where they could show off certain projects they had been working on throughout the year. During that activity, she showed how she had re-decorated her room with pictures of Christ on her walls. She said, "I used to be tempted to look at pornography in my room, but now I'm not."

What kind of fifteen-year-old is willing to admit that to the other girls? I'll tell you who—one who was championed for repentance and has not been shamed. Good job, Mamma!

There is a story about repentance in the New Testament that I love so much. I love it so much because it's a parable told by Jesus about a repentant son and his father. If I'm going to trust anyone to tell me how His dad, our Father in Heaven, feels, it will be Jesus. Because Jesus knows God the best and knows what He would or wouldn't do in a given situation.

And here's another fun fact that makes what Jesus says about God accurate. Jesus Christ and God are one in purpose. They think the same. They don't disagree with each other. So when Jesus tells a story about His dad, we need to listen up. We know it is 100% correct.

Here, Jesus is eating and chatting with publicans and sinners. Along come the Pharisees and scribes. The Pharisees are the ones keeping the commandments sooo well, remember? They take all the proper steps on Sundays and ensure everyone sees them taking the correct number of steps. And they judge anyone who doesn't do things exactly right like they do. Of course, they start judging Jesus for hanging out with people that they believe are not worthy of attention or love. And Christ, being ever ready to teach them, sees an opportunity. He wants to teach these self-righteous people that everyone is important to God. Every single person. But to get His point across in a non-confrontational way, He will tell them a story—a parable.

I love parables. I enjoy them because they take some thinking. *How does this story apply to me?* Christ probably liked to tell them too, because He wants us to use our minds. He likes to tell us stuff and then let the Spirit teach us what it means for us. Sometimes Christ's teachings are like puzzles. Have you ever tried the puzzle with the two nails that are bent together, and you turn it round and round, and it isn't until you get it in just the correct position that you see the answer on how to get them apart? Once you figure it out, it's easy to do it again and again.

Christ taught like this when He was on the earth. His gospel is simple; you just have to look at it correctly. You have to turn it round and round in your mind until it lines upright. And you get the added bonus of the Spirit saying, "Now just turn it a tiny bit more to the right."

I like the process. When the Lord uses the scriptures to teach me how to live and apply them to my life, it's pretty cool.

But back to Christ's lunch with the sinners and the hoity-toity Pharisees. He starts easily by giving them an example that most will understand: sheep. These people know sheep. They feed them. They eat them. They sacrifice them. It feels familiar.

He asks them a straightforward question. If a man lost a sheep, wouldn't he leave all the others and go find it? And when he finds it, wouldn't he go show everyone and tell everyone how happy he was that he found it?

Maybe there is silence. Maybe some people look confused. Maybe that's why Christ just gives them the interpretation right there. He tells them that there will be so much joy in heaven over that one person that repents more than all the ones that don't need to repent!

Are they getting it now? I'm not so sure.

He tells them about a woman who has ten pieces of silver, and she loses one. She searches everywhere until she finds it. She calls the neighbors and tells them all she found it, and they all rejoice together.

Do you see this scene in your mind? Everyone is jumping in a circle in her entryway, chanting, "You found your coin. Woo hoo! You found your coin." She must have had cool neighbors.

In this example, Christ in essence said, "Now do you get it? This is how heaven feels when one person repents!"

Silence. Maybe a cricket chirps in the background.

This is me playing the scene out. He may tell three different stories to illustrate the same point because there are shepherds and old ladies that need the message in a way they would personally understand. But in my mind, it looks a bit different. I think they just aren't getting it. So, He stops talking about animals and silver and starts talking about people. "Maybe you don't care about sheep or a few coins. But maybe you can put yourself in the place of a child." Every single person in that room understood being a child of someone.

He tells them a story about a man who has two sons. One of them gets bored living at home, so he asks for his inheritance early to go live the high life somewhere else. I read an article the other day that said because of the customs of the day, this son said, "I wish you were dead." That is when children got inheritances back then—when their fathers died.

Ouch.

It is interesting to note here that the dad gave him his inheritance. He didn't say, "Maybe when you're older or smarter." Or, "No way! You'll just waste it." Or "What? You want me dead? Rude!" We need to observe that the dad just gives it to him and lets him make his own choices. This is one of the greatest gifts our Heavenly Father gives to us—agency. He doesn't force us to do anything, even if He knows we will make a mess out of things, or it isn't a great idea. He can't. It is against His nature. He lets us do what we want.

The scriptures say, "Not many days after the younger son gathered all together and took his journey into the far country, and there wasted his substance with riotous living" (Luke 15:13). We really don't know what "riotous living" is, but we can probably guess. This son blows all his money, and to add insult to injury, right then, a famine hits the land. He's out of money and needs to get more. He's hungry.

It says he finds a job that includes feeding pigs. But obviously, he isn't getting significantly paid for this mundane task because we read that one day, he is so hungry that he thinks about eating the pig slop. Blech. He must have been starving!

The story then says, "he came to himself" (Luke 15:17). I'm not exactly sure what this means, but I think it means that he woke up. He gets an idea. This son is ready to eat the pig's dinner when he thinks, *My dad's servants are eating way better than this. I know. I'll go to my dad and say, "I'm not worthy to be your son anymore because I am a loser, a sinner. I wasted your money. I made bad choices. I'm sorry. I know I don't deserve to be in your house, but can I be one of your servants?"*

He's feeling really bad. He is sorry.

Can you imagine how that son feels walking home? He really has to humble himself to turn to his dad and tell him he wasted all his money and that he'd made a mess of things. I'm sure that is one, long walk.

Now, we are getting to the part that is important for us to digest when trying to understand the nature of our Heavenly Father. "But when he was yet a great way off, his father saw him and had compassion and ran and fell on his neck and kissed him" (Luke 15:20).

Think about the phrase, "yet a great way off." Think about that. His dad is watching for him! His dad isn't in the barn tending the cows or sitting on the porch reading the paper. He watches for him and looks down the road, waiting and hoping that he would come home. Heavenly Father is always watching for us, even when we're far away.

And then it says he runs to him. He doesn't stand in the driveway with his arms folded, waiting for his son to make the agonizing walk up the drive. No, he runs to meet his repentant son! Remember the primary source that is telling this story. It's Christ. He is telling us about the nature of his Father—our Father. He's describing what they both would do because they are one in purpose, remember?

"And the son said unto him, Father, I have sinned against heaven and in thy sight, and I am no more worthy to be called thy son" (Luke 15:21). He says it just as he has rehearsed it.

What did the dad do next? The father doesn't even address what the kid says. He turns and says to his servants:

> "Bring forth the best robe and put it on him and put a ring on his hand and shoes on his feet, and bring hither that fatted calf and kill it and let us eat and be merry. For my son was dead and is alive again. He was lost and is found." And they began to be merry (Luke 15:22-23).

That dad never says, "See, I told you, you'd be back. I knew you wouldn't make it. It's about time you came crawling back." He is just happy he is back.

He is just happy.

That's how Heavenly Father reacts when we come to ourselves. That's how He acts when we turn around and start the long walk home. Don't forget this. It's true. Jesus said so.

But the story isn't quite done. Jesus may look around the room at this point and see the glistening eyes of so many sinners. He feels that many people now understood God's amazing love for them. But there are a few—probably some of the judgmental Pharisees—thinking, *Well, that's not fair! What about the other son who did everything right? Where was his party? He's the one who deserved it. Not the kid who blew the money.* Christ continues because He wants everyone in the room to understand the weight that Heavenly Father puts on repentance.

He explains that the other son was in the field when he heard about the party. It doesn't say what he was doing in the field, but we assume it was working. Dutiful son doing the dutiful things, right? Christ may have wanted to say, "Hey Pharisees ... this is you. The one who thinks he's done everything right. He's taken all the right steps on all the right days. He's never wasted any of the money."

Perfect son.

Well, not quite. Because it says that the other son calls one of the servants and asks what is going on.

"Why the party?"

The servant says, "Thy brother is come; and thy father hath killed the fatted calf, because he hath received him safe and sound" (Luke 15:27).

Christ continues, "And he (this perfect brother) was angry, and would not go in" (Luke 15:28). Why was this brother mad? Why wasn't he happy that his brother was safe? Hadn't he worried about him? Hadn't he foreseen the dangers that his dad had seen when he left town? It doesn't look like it to me.

But the following line once again teaches us about God. "And he was angry, and would not go in: therefore came his father out." His dad isn't just aware of the lost son and is taken up in the moment of that joy. No, he is now looking around and worries about the other son. God is always worried about all of us. He wants us all to be happy. He wants us all to be safe.

The older son tells his dad that he's always done what is right, and he's never had a party. And he makes sure to point out that the brother had wasted all his money living with harlots. How did he even know that? Was he guessing? Or was he just assuming? It doesn't matter, though, because he is trying to remind his dad how bad his brother is and that he doesn't deserve the party.

Jesus ends the story by lovingly pointing out that all the dad possessed is always available to the righteous son. "Son, thou art ever with me, and all that I have is thine. It was meet that we should make merry, and be glad: for this thy brother was dead, and is alive again; and was lost, and is found" (Luke 15:31-32).

"It was meet that we should make merry." Meet means necessary. "It is necessary to know that you've always done what's right, and you have had and will have all the blessings. But it is also necessary that we should be GLAD that your brother is back. I'm not mad. I'm just so glad. I was so worried."

That's your dad and my dad. That's our Heavenly Father.

And one thing our ever-humble brother, Jesus Christ, didn't mention here is that it is His sacrifice that makes this whole scene possible. Our loving brother paid the price for all our riotous living so that all our Father has to do when we get back home is throw the party.

These are the men anxiously awaiting the opportunity to show you that they are real. The Holy Ghost doesn't work independently. He carries *their* message to you and me. These two are the ones who spoke to my little thirteen-year-old heart and whispered, "We're so sorry you are sad about your clothes. Follow us. Worry more about us than stuff, and you will lead a very rich life, indeed."

When you take this time each day to repent, please think of this father—this guy in the story. Think of the man watching down the road for the son to return. Think of him running out to grab him, hug, and love him, and then throw the party.

Hopefully, that makes it a little easier to clean up your life so that you can have the influence of the Holy Ghost with you consistently. You need it. It will make all the difference in developing your relationship with Heavenly Father and Jesus Christ.

Another significant aspect of repentance is that it gets easier when we do it daily.

I have a glass shower in my bathroom. I have a squeegee in there that I use every time I take a shower. It takes less than a minute when I'm done, and I always have a shiny, clean shower.

But this one part is too thin to get the squeegee into. So, I just don't squeegee that part. And do you know what? I can no longer see through that section of glass. It's been covered over by hard water stains and calcification. Someday, when I find the time and get the motivation, I will have to really work to clean that part up.

It's going to be hard, and it will take time. If only I would have just wiped that little section down every day! I wouldn't be looking that chore in the face every day when I get in the shower.

Suppose we do an accurate inventory of our lives every morning when we sit down before the Lord to read our scriptures. In that case, we are, in essence, squeegeeing our lives every day. Sins don't build upon sins, and we can keep the Spirit with us and keep our lives in check.

The other beautiful thing about repenting and trying to come before the Lord clean every day is that sometimes we don't recognize the little sins we are committing. Sometimes we don't even know when we are starting to head off course. This is why the scriptures are such a blessing to us.

"All scripture is given by inspiration of God, and is profitable for doctrine, for reproof, for correction, for instruction in righteousness" (2 Tim. 3:16).

This is such a great byproduct of studying this way. So often, the Lord will give you a little nudge right where you are reading, letting you know there might be something you need to fix.

I imagine Him saying, "Hey—you missed a spot."

And humility should elicit this response from us every time. "Oh, thanks for looking out for me. You're right. I didn't see it there."

Getting back to the reading plan, I don't want you to dwell on your sins here. Satan gets good at making us feel unworthy to pray, and it shouldn't happen here. When we acknowledge our faults, we clear the air before the Lord and welcome the Holy Ghost.

Christ knows what you've done. He knows how far off the path you've wandered. You don't have to go into detail, maybe just, "I'm sorry for not being my best lately." That will suffice. Don't get stuck here.

Your two-hour Enos-in-the-woods repentance prayer can come later. For now, just admit you aren't perfect and be grateful for Jesus. We are so lucky to have Him.

CHAPTER 12

*"...in every thing by prayer and supplication
with thanksgiving let your requests be made
known unto God. And the peace of God, which
passeth all understanding, shall keep your hearts
and minds through Christ Jesus."*

Philipians 4:6-7

Step 1.3 Ask For Inspiration

There is one last thing you can do during this
prayer. You can tell the Lord what you're worried about or what you want. Ask Him to help you
find answers to your predicament, guidance in your
choices, or just to feel His love.

Many days my prayer doesn't involve this step;
I simply ask to learn *something*. Sometimes I don't
have some big pressing problem or concern—I'm
reading just to be obedient. The most remarkable
thing happens these days too. I always learn something. It's always fun to see what the Lord has for
me each day.

But sometimes, I go to the Lord with a specific question, and then I read, cross-reference, pray some more, and repeat this pattern again and again, until I get an answer.

For example, in the beginning of 2020, I had some big decisions to make. I had met my soon-to-be second husband, and we were trying to figure out if we could afford to get married. He was still supporting his ex-wife financially, and I was living on my alimony from my ex-husband. If we married, we would have to maintain two homes in two different states and all the expenses that would incur, not to mention the cost of flying back and forth every week between Georgia and Arizona. If I remarried, my alimony would be gone, and it looked as if there was no way we could afford this life.

My podcast, "Come Follow Me for Us," was in full swing, and I had actually started a second podcast, "The Book of Mormon for Youth," that I later handed off to my sister. I was also the Young Women's president of my ward at the time. I hardly had any extra time and didn't know what to do. Where could I find a job that I could do in two different states? What about this book that I felt so prompted to write? I thought about it all the time. I talked through options and really tried to figure out the best plan.

I finally decided to take it to the Lord. I started praying, reading, pondering, and writing: this went on for hours. All my flaws and inadequacies floated to the top as I read. Scripture after scripture prompted me to repent. As I continued to read, I began to feel more and more remorseful for some things

I had a bad attitude about. I really felt the need for forgiveness. I studied all day long. Finally, I somehow ended up in the 25th Section of the Doctrine and Covenants. Many of the feelings and revelations that I got that day about the whole situation are too personal to share, but I do want to share a portion of what I found and what I wrote.

"Hearken unto the voice of the Lord your God, while I speak unto you, *(Melanie, my daughter;)* for verily I say unto you, all those who receive my gospel are sons and daughters in my kingdom. A revelation I give unto you concerning my will; and if thou art faithful and walk in the paths of virtue before me, I will preserve thy life, and thou shalt receive an inheritance in Zion. Behold, thy sins are forgiven thee, and thou art an elect lady, whom I have called."

I've been begging for forgiveness today and the ability to go forward in faith!! So many tears!!

"Murmur not because of the things which thou hast not seen, for they are withheld from thee which is wisdom in me in a time to come."

So don't worry that you don't have all the answers now. They'll come.

"... and thy time shall be given to writing, and to learning much."

Wow! Write that book. No more direct message than that!

"And thou needest not fear, for thy husband shall support thee ..." (Doctrine and Covenants 25:1-4, 8-9).

Can you believe it? Right there—write your book, and your husband will support you. The two things I was worried about the most were right there, in the same chapter. I didn't get there by looking up writing or husband in the topical guide. I got there by jumping from scripture to scripture and conference talk to conference talk all day. I kept reading and praying and following the influence of the Spirit until the Lord revealed His will to me in this matter. I say over and over, "The Lord knows where all the words are." And He does! We just have to have faith in the process and not give up. We have to return again and again until we learn to recognize His voice.

Be patient at the beginning of this process. Learning to hear His voice takes practice. Every day when you turn to the Lord in the scriptures, imagine yourself shooting baskets into the old hoop above the garage. Every day you shoot, you get better and better at it. It takes work. It takes persistence. But the more you study and learn, the more proficient you will get. For every shot that lands just right, you'll want to return again and again. It will stop feeling like work and will become fun. It will become rewarding. You will want to return again and again.

At the end of studying that day, I wrote, *Thank you, Heavenly Father and Jesus Christ. Thank you for always revealing Your will in my life in such specific ways. Please give me the strength to do what I read here.*

I did go forward. I took a scary leap and decided to marry a man who lived across the country. I wasn't sure how it would all work out, but I knew that it was the will of the Lord. I trusted and moved forward, and the Lord worked out the details. It was the best decision I ever made.

In Hebrews 4:12, we read, "For the word of God is quick, and powerful, and sharper than any two-edged sword, piercing even to the dividing asunder of soul and spirit, and of the joints and marrow, and is a discerner of the thoughts and intents of the heart." This is one of my favorite things about turning to the scriptures for inspiration. When my mind is confused or troubled, like it was about marrying Shane, I can turn to the scriptures to help me discern the thoughts and intents of my heart. It's such a gift from God.

Most of the other translations of the Bible begin this verse by saying that the word of God is *"living and active" (ESV),* and *"alive and powerful" (NLT).* In the Aramaic Bible, in plain English, it says, *"living and all-efficient."* This is because the Greek word for *quick* means "alive, living, lively." The Greek word for *powerful* means "full of energy, energized, active, effective." I love this. LOVE THIS!

Because it isn't the scriptures discerning our thoughts and hearts, it's the Lord. Don't forget this. Inspiration comes to us from God and the Savior through the power of the Holy Ghost. Remember,

"In the beginning was the Word, and the Word was with God, and the Word was God" (John 1:1).

Who was with God in the beginning? Jesus Christ.

Did we miss that somehow? This isn't a big secret. That's just a fancy way of saying, "Read this, and you will hear His voice because all of this is His voice."

This is one way He can communicate with us. These aren't old words written long ago for a group of people no longer here. They are for us right now. They are alive, powerful, and efficient. This is why this method of "Hearing Him" is so effective.

This scripture in Hebrews mentions two-edged swords, which is a sword that is sharp on both sides. It can slice through just about anything. It can slice through pride and doubt. It can cut through ignorance and sin. Trust me; I don't just hear fluffy platitudes from the Lord when I search for His voice. Truth is, I often get chastened and told I need to change. It's not always fun for God to call you a Lemuel and tell you to quit complaining. It's not fun to have God say, "Why haven't you been doing what I asked? What is holding you back?" But it's so important.

In the book of Helaman, we read:

> Yea, we see that *whosoever will* may lay hold upon the word of God, which is quick and powerful, which shall divide asunder all the cunning and the snares and the wiles of the devil, and lead the man of Christ in a strait and narrow course across that everlasting gulf of misery which is prepared to engulf the wicked— And land their

souls, yea, their immortal souls, at the right hand of God in the kingdom of heaven, ... to go no more out (Helaman 3:29-30).

Not only will the word of God help us figure out our own thoughts, but it will also show us where Satan is trying to trip us up. This is imperative for our spiritual survival. Lawrence Corbridge stated:

There are many who deceive, and the spectrum of deception is broad. At one end we meet those who attack the Restoration, the Prophet Joseph Smith, and the Book of Mormon. Next we see those who believe in the Restoration but claim the Church is deficient and has gone astray. There are others who also claim to believe in the Restoration but are disillusioned with doctrine that conflicts with the shifting attitudes of our day. There are some who, without authority, lay claim to visions, dreams, and visitations to right the ship, guide us to a higher path, or prepare the Church for the end of the world. Others are deceived by false spirits.

At the far end of the spectrum we come to an entire universe of distractions. Never has there been more information, misinformation, and disinformation; more goods, gadgets, and games; and more options, places to go, and things to see and do to occupy time and attention away from what is most important. And all of that and much more is disseminated instantaneously throughout the world by electronic media. *This is a day of deception (emphasis added).*[25]

Amen! What he said.

How do we get through this life without being deceived? How do we sift through all of that information and know what is real and what isn't? We turn to the word of God with our questions. We turn to the word of God when we have doubts. We turn to the word of God when we are angry, sad, or frustrated. This tool is available to all of us. Helaman couldn't have been clearer when he stated, "Whosoever will may lay hold upon the word of God," (Helaman 3:19).

Any of us can have our questions answered. God wants to lead and direct every one of us. He wants us all to return to Him, safe and sound.

But we have to choose Him. We have to go to the source.

CHAPTER 13

*"Whosoever drinketh of the water that I shall
give him shall never thirst; but the water that
I shall give him shall be in him a well of water
springing up into everlasting life."*

John 4:13-14

When I was a kid, my mom and my siblings spent a few weeks every summer at my mom's family cabin up South Fork Canyon in Ogden, Utah. It sits on the banks of a river wide and deep enough to float down on inner tubes. The cabin itself can't be more than 1,000 square feet. It can't be, and yet, you should see how many of us we have shoved in there. There is a sign on the wall above one of the beds that says, "Six persons per bed limit!" I'm not kidding.

There is also a sign by the bathroom that says, "How long a minute is depends on what side of the door you're on." Another one on the counter when you walk in says, "This place is kind of a dump, but the people are friendly."

There are three couches shoved into the only room that isn't a bedroom. None of them match. Two of them touch each other. One is pre-1975, I guarantee. There are videotapes and a VCR, and dominoes in a metal lunch box.

This cabin belonged to my grandparents. When my grandparents were still alive, the two of them and I would sit in the front seat of their Chevette and make bets as to how many cars we would pass on the way in or out of the canyon. They had a plastic "clicker" which we would use to count every car that passed us. Whoever was the closest to the correct answer got a prize. It was usually a quarter, sometimes even a 50-cent piece, and I swear I once got a whole dollar. They were the coolest grandparents, and my summers with them were a total treat.

My grandpa died when I was in eighth grade. I don't have a lot of memories with him, but one thing I vividly remember is how he made me feel. I felt loved and important and valued by him. He was always happy to see me and would throw his arms out wide and exclaim, as he saw me get out of the car, "There's my Melanie!"

How grateful I am that when I think of him, in place of specifics, I get a feeling. This same kind of reminiscing can be applied to my Father in Heaven. I don't have specific memories of before I came to earth, but I do know how I feel when I think about my Heavenly Father. I think that sensitivity trailed me to earth and has surrounded me since the day I was born.

Because my grandfather died when I was only twelve, most of my memories from when I was young at the cabin revolve around my grandmother. She loved to tell us stories. I would lie in the big, bouncy bed in the step-down room, my hands absent-mindedly playing with the little colored balls on the chenille comforter as she shared one crazy story after another from memory.

They often involved magical woods, fairies, spells, trolls, and the like. The characters were so colorful, and her stories so descriptive you couldn't help but look at butterflies, moss, bridges, and rainbows differently after spending time with her. With pride, I can say she helped color my world when I was a child. She filled me with wonder and imagination, candied popcorn balls and Pepsi® from glass bottles. She taught us to "zip" white horses, play cards, and read books. I think through her storytelling, I learned the magic of words and how they touch us. I also learned to never give up hope too early in the story, especially when all looks lost.

We would often go on hikes when we would visit in the summers—my favorite one being up above Causey Dam. There used to be a boy scout camp called Camp Keisel that we would walk around and then head up to the top of the mountain. The dusty road eventually narrowed to a path that narrowed even further to a small trail that meandered in and out of the shade. Wildlife scampered around us the whole way.

It felt magical up there.

The best part about this hike was that if you endured long enough and made it to the very top, you could get to the place where the water that filled the dam basically came out of the ground. The spring.

You could dip your hands in that freezing water and get a drink of the purest water around. It was the best after a long, hot hike.

One time, on a particularly hot day, some of us got really tired and didn't want to traverse all the way to the top. We decided we were far enough up to go ahead and take a drink. We went to the edge of the stream and dipped our hands in the cool, refreshing water and drank and drank.

A few kids scrambled up a little further; pretty soon, us lazier ones who had stopped to drink heard a scream.

"Gross!! Ahhh!!"

Of course that meant something awesome that we all had to see. When we got to where the rest of the kids were, we noticed what the commotion was all about. Right there, lying in the very middle of the water, directly above where we had been drinking, was a dead, rotting deer.

Immediately we realized that along with that refreshing sip, we probably also got a gulp or two of dead deer water! As I write, I swear I can still smell it.

I've thought about that day again and again, especially when I think about spiritual things and where to turn when I have questions or concerns. I have to make sure I go to the source, or else I run the risk of getting a mouthful of giardia and perhaps getting really sick, or worse.

Our Heavenly Father has promised us access to Him. The heavens are not closed. We don't have to stumble through this life alone. There is a spring gushing forth with knowledge and purity and clarity, and it's available to all of us, dead-deer free!

We've been promised. "Whosoever drinketh of the water that I shall give him shall never thirst; but the water that I shall give him shall be in him a well of water springing up into everlasting life" (John 4:13-14).

CHAPTER 14

"By pondering, we give the Spirit an opportunity to impress and direct. Pondering is a powerful link between the heart and the mind. As we read the scriptures, our hearts and minds are touched. If we use the gift to ponder, we can take these eternal truths and realize how we can incorporate them into our daily actions."

Elder Marvin J. Ashton

Step 2 and 3 Read and Ponder

Wow. It's taking us a minute to get through these steps, huh?

As I said, you are not putting any chapter constraints on your daily reading. You are reading for an amount of *time*, not a certain number of *verses or chapters*.

As you read, take a few moments here and there to stop and think about what you are reading. Ask yourself some questions. "How does this apply to my life?" "What can I learn from this?" "Is there something the Lord wants me to learn in these passages?"

President Benson said in his talk, "The Book of Mormon—Keystone of our Religion," that the Book of Mormon was written for our day. He testified that different prophets thought about us as they decided what to include and what to leave out. He then says:

> If they saw our day and chose those things which would be of greatest worth to us, is not that how we should study the Book of Mormon? We should constantly ask ourselves, "Why did the Lord inspire Mormon (or Moroni or Alma) to include that in his record? What lesson can I learn from that to help me live in this day and age?[26]

Pondering is such an important part of this process. Nephi testifies that as he sat pondering the things that his father had told him about the Tree of Life, he was "caught away in the spirit of the Lord" (1 Nephi 11:1). He was then taken to see all his father saw, PLUS he asked for an interpretation of it all. His pondering led to the inspired interpretation of the dream of the Tree of Life.

When Christ was WITH THE NEPHITES, preaching to them daily, He admonished them to go home and ponder in their hearts the things that He had told them. He then told them to "...ask of the Father, in my name, that ye may understand, and prepare your minds for the morrow, and I come unto you again" (3 Nephi 17:3).

I imagine Him saying, "I've told you a lot. It's hard for you to get it all right now. So go home and think about it for a while. Ask your Heavenly Father to help you digest what I said. Ask Him to show you how My words apply to your life. Yes, you, personally. And then ask Him to prepare your mind to hear what I have to say to you tomorrow."

You would think that hearing something straight from Christ's mouth would be enough, but even Christ knew the power of pondering. Christ knew that as they thought about His words, as they mulled over His teachings, the Holy Ghost would confirm the truth of it to them. He knew the Holy Ghost would carry what they needed to know independently to their very hearts in a powerful way. Pondering invites the Lord to customize His message just for us.

I think of Moroni's words, uttered at the very end of the Book of Mormon right before he sealed up the record and hid it in the earth; sometimes it's referred to as "Moroni's Promise." Most of the time, we start in verse four of chapter 10. But why do we skip verse three?

> Behold, I would exhort you that when ye shall read these things, if it be wisdom in God that ye should read them, that ye would remember how merciful the Lord hath been unto the children of men, from the creation of Adam even down until the time that ye shall receive these things, and ponder it in your hearts.

And *then* he asks us to pray and ask if the Book of Mormon is true in verse four. *Then* he speaks these beautiful words "by the power of the Holy Ghost we shall know the truth of all things" (Moroni 10:3-4).

Why do you think it's so important to ponder all the miracles that God has poured out on the children of men *before* you kneel down to ask if the Book of Mormon really is the word of God?

Because when we ponder about and remember all that God has done for us, we open up the channels of heaven.

Elder Marvin J. Ashton taught:

> By pondering, we give the Spirit an opportunity to impress and direct. Pondering is a powerful link between the heart and the mind. As we read the scriptures, our hearts and minds are touched. If we use the gift to ponder, we can take these eternal truths and realize how we can incorporate them into our daily actions.[27]

President Monson said, "I implore each of us to prayerfully study and ponder the Book of Mormon each day. As we do so, we will be in a position to hear the voice of the Spirit, to resist temptation, to overcome doubt and fear, and to receive heaven's help in our lives."[28]

Notice he didn't just say read; he said to study and *ponder*. We have been told over and over to read the scriptures, and so many of us do that.

Check, following that commandment.

But I think most of us don't understand the value of pondering. This is where the cool stuff starts happening, and this is why my mission president's method is so simple, but so powerful.

When we pray, repent, and show gratitude, we, in essence, knock on the Lord's door and let Him know we are there and want to receive communication.

And then we start reading. We read a little and think a little.

Read, pause, think. Read, pause, think.

And then things start happening! Cool things. Like Liahona cool!

About a month after I got to Japan, Elder Haun of the Quorum of the Seventy came to Kyoto to preside over our stake conference. In the evening session, he called me and another elder who had just begun our missions to come up and bear our testimonies. I thought he had lost his mind. I could pretty much say, "I love God," and "I threw up yesterday in the cafeteria." How in the world would I be able to express my thoughts to *all these people* IN JAPANESE?! I got up and began by saying, "My heart is full." I had never put those words in combination before, and as I spoke, I was able to say the things of my heart. It was short and to the point, but I was able to say basically what I felt. One of our investigators came up to me afterward and said, "I really liked your speech." I had actually said words that made sense to a room full of people. Indeed, my heart was full.

That experience gave me hope that one day I would be able to share what I wanted with the people of Japan—using actual words.

We studied and practiced teaching the discussions, and when we thought we had mastered each one, we had to pass them off to our district leader. One time, I was sitting in the back of the chapel, passing off one of the lessons with our district leader. Right when I got to the part where I had to share my feelings about Jesus Christ, a small earthquake shook the tiny chapel. As the lights swayed back and forth, Elder Jones said, "If your testimony can shake the earth, I guess you pass."

But despite these few little wins, basically, I was mute. I couldn't understand much of what was being said and could say even less. I was sad. I had always wanted to be a missionary, and now was my chance. And yet, discussion after discussion, I sat silently as my trainer, Sister Wilder, taught the lessons. Sister Wilder was amazing and really tried to help me participate. But she and our investigators would talk and talk, and then she would turn to me and say, "How do you feel about Joseph Smith?" And I would say, "I know that he was a prophet, and I love him," or something to that effect. The Spirit would whoosh into the room, and I felt that God was magnifying the few things I could say, but still, I was discouraged. Sometimes I could hardly even stay awake during our discussions because the conversation between my companion and our investigators just sounded like babbling to me. I felt so lonely in those rooms full of people.

One morning, not long after my mission president had introduced this new way of reading the Book of Mormon, I was studying in 1 Nephi 17. Nephi and his family had been traveling in the wilderness for quite some time—eight years, to be exact. As was mentioned earlier, they had miraculously come to possess the Liahona, which was guiding them in their journey.

At this point, they had arrived at a seashore. Nephi explained that even though the journey had been rough, and they had endured many hardships, they were super happy to have made it to this land. It was full of fruit and wild honey. And remember, they had basically been eating deer sushi for years because the Lord had been making their meat sweet so that they didn't have to cook it. So, when they got to fruit and honey land, they were pretty happy.

After they had been there a little while, the Lord came and told Nephi that he needed to build a boat. I can't even imagine what Nephi thought about this new request. *How am I supposed to build a boat? I came from Jerusalem, remember? I've never even been on a boat. And now you expect me to build one from scratch?* But Nephi was Nephi, remember? So instead of being snarky, he simply asked the Lord how he was supposed to do it.

The Lord taught him how to start a fire with two stones, make bellows to get the fire nice and hot, and then showed him where to get ore to molten into tools. After he got the tools and instructions, he then went and asked his brothers for some help. Laman and Lemuel said, "Sure! We love helping you. You are so smart, and we love getting instructions from our little brother on how to do things."

Just kidding. What they actually said was something like, "Our brother is a fool. He thinks he can build a ship, but that's a joke. And the bigger joke is that he thinks we can cross those big ol' waters. The funniest thing of all is Nephi thinks the Lord is telling him to do this. Ha ha. The Lord doesn't speak to Nephi." And they went on like this, murmuring like always. I think Laman probably kicked some sand on Nephi as he walked away.

Do you think that Nephi wanted to scream here? "Are you kidding me, people? The Lord IS guiding me. He told us to go get the plates, and we tried and failed the first time. Then we were in that cave, and you guys were beating me with that rod when an actual angel came and stopped you. Then I cut off Laban's head, remember? Remember that deal with the broken bow and the Liahona? What about not needing fire all these years because God has been leading us by His light in the nighttime and making our meat safe to eat without cooking it? Do you even appreciate this deer sushi anymore, or have you forgotten who's making it for us?"

Nephi got really sad. And when his brothers saw him get sad, they got really happy. It actually says that they rejoiced. And then they mocked him by saying, "We knew that ye could not construct a ship, for we knew that ye were lacking in judgement; wherefore, thou canst not accomplish so great a work" (1 Nephi 17:19).

They went on and on, telling Nephi he was like their dumb dad who yanked them away from all their money and stuff, and made them wander in the wilderness for years and waaah waah, grumble, murmur.

What Nephi did next is cool. He reminded them of what the Lord did for Moses and his people in the scriptures. I love that he told them the story of Moses. I think we should do this more with our children. It's likening the scriptures to us, and it's powerful. It's how Alma taught King Lamoni, and I dig it.

But Nephi basically told them that the Lord provides a way for those who follow Him and keep His commandments. He also told them about how Moses led the people and saved them from the fiery serpents. And then he told them what happened to the jerks who hardened their hearts against Moses and the Lord. He went on to tell them they weren't doing what they were supposed to be doing, and that he was afraid if they didn't straighten up, they were going to be in deep trouble.

They didn't love this speech and decided to grab him and throw him in the ocean and drown him. Nephi then spoke with the power of God and told them that he had indeed been commanded of God to build the ship. And if they touched him that they would literally "wither even as a dried reed ... for God shall smite [them]" (1 Nephi 17:48). He told them to stop murmuring against their dad and God, and that they needed to get to work and help him.

Then Nephi says this, "And now, if the Lord has such great power, and has wrought so many miracles among the children of men, how is it that he cannot instruct me that I should build a ship?" (1 Nephi 27:49).

When I read those words, the spirit of the Lord filled my little apartment in Japan. I stopped and started pondering and thinking about how this story and those words applied to my life.

I felt the Lord saying these words to me. "Melanie, you have seen so many miracles in your life! Your dad was miraculously healed from cancer four years ago. You know of this power. You know what I can do. Do you really think I can't instruct you to learn Japanese?"

I thought back to the many miracles I had seen in my lifetime, and also to the miracles that Jesus Christ performed in the Bible. Christ raised people from the dead, healed withered hands, and softened hearts. Certainly, helping me learn Japanese would be easy compared to that.

I wrote in my journal that morning, *I do not need to see an angel or hear the voice of the Lord. I am hearing it plain as day in the pages of the Book of Mormon!* I was again flooded with the same feelings of love that I felt the night the Lord comforted me about GUESS® jeans. The Lord knew me. He was aware of my situation, and I was learning to hear His voice in a powerful, undeniable way.

President Nelson recently said:

> My dear brothers and sisters, I promise that as you prayerfully study the Book of Mormon every day, you will make better decisions—every day. I promise that as you ponder what you study, the windows of heaven will open, and you will receive answers to your own questions and direction for your own life.[29]

CHAPTER 15

"There is something eternal in the very nature of writing, as is so graphically illustrated by the scriptures themselves. In a very real sense, our properly written histories are a very important part of our family scripture and become a great source of spiritual strength to us and to our posterity."

John H. Groberg

Step 4 Write

Write down the scriptures that stand out to you and why they do. This part is great for lots of reasons.

First, this daily study becomes a spiritual journal of your life. You are keeping a record of the Lord's communications with you and your insights and inspired answers to prayers. If faithfully kept and preserved, one day, one of your progenitors may find answers to their prayers through something the Lord taught you many, many years before. The Lord loves to do this. He does it all over through the scriptures. He will answer the prayers of a person or group of people, and their experience blesses you and teaches you what you need to know.

Likewise, the lessons you learn will, one day, have the ability to teach your people the things they need to know when they need it most. My friend Emily once said to me, "The Lord is often answering many prayers simultaneously." Maybe He knows that one of your grandkids will have a rough day in the future, and something that He teaches you today will bless *her* tomorrow.

It's a two-for-one. He loves two-for-ones!

John H. Groberg said:

> There is something eternal in the very nature of writing, as is so graphically illustrated by the scriptures themselves. In a very real sense, our properly written histories are a very important part of our family scripture and become a great source of spiritual strength to us and to our posterity.[30]

Deuteronomy 4:9 teaches an important truth: "Only take heed to thyself, and keep thy soul diligently, lest thou forget the things which thine eyes have seen, and lest they depart from thy heart all the days of thy life: but teach them thy sons, and thy sons' sons." How are we going to remember all the things and ways the Lord has blessed our lives? By writing them down! Someday I hope my years of scripture journals will bless my posterity. It's not going to be super fun for me when they read the reprimands I got from above—the times that I was wrong, and God let me know it. But it's ok; I'll be dead. If they judge me too hard, I'll knock a vase off the shelf or flick the lights on and off in their closets when they are trying to sleep. That'll show 'em not to judge me.

My friend said, "I think there is so much value in being honest about what we write. If our journals are sugar-coated, our posterity will wonder why we never went through hard times, but they have to. It's the same thing for me as I learn about really hard things in church history. It actually allows me to love those people more BECAUSE things were so hard, and they struggled so much. The fact that Emma went through so many hard things, resisted some of them, and served and loved everyone while suffering is why I love her so much and why her example has helped me so much. I think our posterity will love us more and actually judge us less if we are honest in our writings."

Nephi talked about why he wrote down the thoughts he had while pondering in 2 Nephi 4:15, "And upon these, I write the things of my soul, ... For my soul delighteth in the scriptures, and my heart pondereth them, and writeth them for the learning and the profit of my children." Nephi was thinking about his children as he wrote.

Good idea, Nephi.

The other thing that the Lord loves to do is let us teach ourselves. That sounds like it makes no sense, but it does. Here's what I mean. When we go back and read our journals—our dealings with the Lord—

sometimes He uses our own experiences to teach us again and again. In the real world, with our finite minds and busy schedules, and information coming at us one thousand miles a minute, we tend to forget important things.

We forget experiences and answers to prayers that we have received. We forget the way we felt when God manifested Himself to us. We forget so much. But if we have it written down, in our own words, we can turn back and have the blessing of feeling all the feels again and again. It's fantastic when we can teach ourselves something new—that really isn't new at all.

It's hilarious to me sometimes to go back and listen to my old podcast episodes from earlier seasons. Sometimes I'll hear myself say something that I think is profound or good. And I'll say to myself, "Wow! I never thought of that like that before." Hahaha. So quickly, we forget. Writing down our experiences helps us to do the vital task of remembering.

Another aspect of writing things down is that it helps our minds to focus. Because of my ADHD, my mind is constantly on the move. I jump from one thought to the next so fast that it makes my head hurt sometimes.

I may sit down to read the scriptures, but as soon as I start to read, I hear a sound outside and remember that I need to go check if the hose is turned off. Then my mind will go to the water that may have been left on and then to the water bill, and I will wonder if I put it on autopay or not. When I think that, I think that I need to check, but my computer is dead, and I don't remember where I put the cord. When I think of the word "dead," I then think of which kid left the water on and how I will punish them. Then I think of how many jobs need to be done around the house and how good it will be to have a kid who owes me big time for leaving the hose on. On and on.

After twenty minutes of that kind of thinking, I realize that I've finished my reading for the night, not having processed anything that I read. It's the folly of my busy brain, but it's also one of Satan's favorite things to do. He loves to throw us off track and make us not focus on what is essential. He's good at it, but not good enough to conquer pondering and writing down. It keeps you focused; it keeps the revelation flowing.

On my mission and throughout most of my life, I have kept physical paper journals. I would read for a bit, and when something stood out to me, I would write that scripture down in my journal and what I felt about it. I have volumes of these journals. Sometimes they were pretty and color-coded and organized. In some parts of my life, they were scribbled on after the fact by my children. But no matter how good they looked, they always helped me ponder. They helped me keep my mind on the words of life, and they are chockful of revelation given to me in critical times of my life. They are treasures.

Then along came technology and the ability to read the scriptures on my phone. This was awesome because I had my phone with me all the time. I could read in the pickup line or waiting for the doctor. I could read anywhere.

In the gospel library app, you can take notes and cross-reference so easily. It makes finding answers so much faster. You can jump from scripture to scripture and end up in conference talks and hymns and even in BYU speeches in mere seconds. Our Savior can get messages to us quicker and easier than ever before. We can write down our feelings right there in the app, and years later, when you're reading that same verse, you can click on the note you see that you wrote and be reminded of how the Lord used that same scripture to teach you things before. It's so handy.

You can also tag scriptures and talks you read with keywords for later study. There are so many fun things technology can do. I like to read this way and do so when I don't have a lot of time, or I'm in a place where I can't sit and write in a notebook or on my computer.

There are two small drawbacks I see to this method. First, I haven't found a way to export my thoughts from the app to save them as a journal. There may be a way I haven't figured out, or the church may come up with one, but for now, that's unfortunate. And second, you're on your phone. Not everyone is as distractible as me, so reading on your phone may not be as big of a problem for you as it is for me. As soon as I open my phone to try to communicate with the Lord, inevitably, I will get a text, a phone call, or things will begin to pop up on my phone. "You haven't played this game in two hours." Or I think, *Maybe I should just check my email one more time before I read to see if something important has shown up.*

And thirty minutes later, I won't have read a thing. It's the pits. Our phones are remarkable and evil all in one. I can only imagine what my life would look like without a phone. New businesses established, multiple podcasts published, books written lining the shelves, perfectly manicured yard and house. I probably would have even served every person in my neighborhood and maybe even come up with the answer to global warming. But instead, I completed that 20/40 game, looked for cars and houses that I didn't need, and designed many five-star virtual rooms. I've traveled down many YouTube rabbit holes that started with a Google search of how to fix my garbage disposal and ended up hours later, garbage disposal still broken, sitting on the floor of the kitchen watching cucumbers scare the heck out of cats. If I had a dollar for every hour I wasted on social media, I would have enough dollars to buy the luxury car my husband is dreaming of. My phone kills me every day. It is my master, and I mostly hate its beautiful, tempting guts.

With that, I suggest that if you choose to read your scriptures on your phone, which is really handy, you put it on airplane mode before you start. Turn off the notifications that remind you to play a game or tell you that you have a message on Instagram that you need to read right now. Let your phone be the fantastic vehicle it can be to quickly get you to the answers and directions that the Lord wants you to find.

If you can.

It appears I can't. I'm a simple human that has so little self-control. I have learned the best way to keep focused and keep a record of my study is to use my laptop.

This is the way that I do it.

I set aside twenty minutes each day to read. I'm not always perfect, and sometimes my reading goes back and forth between phone and computer. But when I take the time to sit at the computer, free from the world's distractions and especially my phone, inspiration flows.

I open www.churchofjesuschrist.org, and I open a word document on my computer called *Daily Scripture Study*. I then go through the steps of this reading plan. I pray, repent, show gratitude, read, copy and paste scriptures that touch me, ponder and then write what I feel about the scriptures.

Copying and pasting the scriptures instead of re-writing them by hand speeds up the process sooo much. It's amazing. I can also cross-reference super easily on the website and doing it this way has blessed my life.

But sometimes I miss writing on paper. I love practicing penmanship and putting a good gel pen to paper. But the speed at which I can write the thought-provoking scriptures down and move straight to pondering and cross-referencing makes using my computer my favorite way to implement this study plan.

There is one foreseeable problem. I'm on a plane every week, and one day when my plane plummets to the earth, all my thoughts and feelings will go with me.

It will probably be for the best, though, because my study isn't always full of pats on the back and praise from the Savior. I've also received my fair share of gentle reminders from the Savior that I shouldn't have done this or that and that I need to repent. Some of my answers are private, and I'm not sure I want them all to be read someday.

I'll have to figure that all out. Maybe I'll make sure it's saved to the cloud and not on my laptop. Maybe every month or so, I'll print out the pages and put them in a notebook. Or perhaps after I finish writing this page, I'll head into the kitchen to get some lunch and see that I need to clean out my fridge before going grocery-shopping. Then I'll think of the candy I want to buy but shouldn't, and then I'll search my cupboards and freezers for any remaining chocolate that may be hidden somewhere, and I'll forget all about how to make my Daily Scripture Study stand the test of time.

That's what it looks like inside my brain.

But the point is, when I take the time to write down what is happening as I ponder the scriptures, my experience becomes so much richer, my mind wanders less, and I have the ability to leave a journal of my communication with the Lord for my posterity.

I want to share a part of my scripture journal from 2007, so you can see what it looks like to write and ponder. The scripture references jump all around, so I was definitely cross-referencing a lot.

October 22, 2007
I just got called yesterday to be the Stake Young Women's president. Right at a time when I was already feeling a little overwhelmed with my life. The Lord gives

me more to do when I need it most so He can bless me more. Someone once said that the opposite of this scripture is also true. "Where much is given, much is required." *So—where much is required, much is given.*

Doctrine and Covenants 64:33:

Wherefore, be not weary in well-doing, for ye are laying the foundation of a great work. And out of small things proceedeth that which is great. Behold, the Lord requireth the heart and a willing mind.

I've been trying lately to have the Lord help change my heart. Now I have to have a willing mind too! Dang it!

Here is some counsel for me in this new calling:

Joshua 22:5

1. *Love the Lord your God.*
2. *Walk in all His ways.*
3. *Keep the commandments.*
4. *Cleave unto Him (cleave means to adhere or stick, to be faithful).*
5. *Serve Him with all your heart and with all your soul!*

Mormon 9:27:

O then despise not and wonder not, but hearken unto the words of the Lord, and ask the Father in the name of Jesus for what things soever ye shall stand in need. Doubt not, but be believing, and begin as in times of old, and come unto the Lord with all your heart.

Remember Virginia! (When I received a hard calling in a brand-new ward, with two small children and a husband almost always absent because of school, the Lord fully sustained me and gave me everything I needed to fulfill that calling.)

I chose this example because it was nothing spectacular. It isn't one of my crazy experiences where the Lord answered me so specifically. But it shows what it looks like to converse with the Lord. It shows how the scriptures are a great discerner of the thoughts and intents of our hearts. And it shows how Christ can give us a game plan. He can offer ideas to help us in whatever is set before us.

I love it. I love working things out with Him every day. I love going back and reading these experiences and seeing just how so many of these things came to pass. Another remarkable miracle I observed, as I read through the journals from this time period, is I saw how I continually came back to the Lord to help me with everything. I needed help with raising my children, that calling, and, eventually, when my spouse at that time left the church. Over and over, I saw myself turning to the Lord instead of the world with my questions and fears. I grew closer to the Lord as my spouse drifted further and further away. Re-reading the words from those years solidified my belief that the Book of Mormon really did save my spiritual life. I don't even want to imagine what would have happened to me if I hadn't been clinging to the word of God through that difficult time. Just like the people in Lehi's dream, I too would have wandered off and been lost had I let go of that iron rod.

<hr/>

*This week I went to a fireside in Georgia where Michelle D. Craig was speaking. She said for us to watch where our minds wander while we are studying the scriptures. Sometimes those things are being put there by our Father in Heaven. I believe that comes with the pondering. But don't entirely disregard the random wanderings. There may be more purpose in them than you realize.

CHAPTER 16

"For if any be a hearer of the word, and not a doer, he is like unto a man beholding his natural face in a glass: For he beholdeth himself, and goeth his way, and straightway forgetteth what manner of man he was."

James 1:23-24

Step 5 Pray Again

When you finish your study for the day, you will say one final prayer. This one is just as important as the first, but sometimes I forget it.

Don't forget.

In this prayer, you will thank Heavenly Father for the time you spent in the scriptures that day. You will thank Him that you have the Book of Mormon to bless your life. Thank Him for the lessons you learned and the revelation that you received. Then pray for the strength to *do what you were prompted to do.*

This is the hardest part for me. Heavenly Father is so good at getting His messages through to me. I hear Christ whisper so many wonderful ideas. I want to go forward and do all the things to bless my family, my neighbors, and everyone else.

And then life happens, and I forget or get distracted. The natural man is so hard to fight. I need all the strength in the world to accomplish all that is expected of me. I need to push Satan and all the distractions out of the way so I can get stuff done. But I need help.

There is a scripture in the New Testament that I love because I think it sums up why this prayer is so necessary.

"For if any be a hearer of the word, and not a doer, he is like unto a man beholding his natural face in a glass: For he beholdeth himself, and goeth his way, and straightway forgetteth what manner of man he was" (James 1:23-24).

Here's my take on this scripture. I read for the day and feel that I need to visit my neighbor and serve her more. I see myself in a lovely red cape with a big basket of treats. I'm humming along as I skip down the street. I knock on her door, go in, and have a lovely visit. She hugs me and tells me my timing is perfect. We both recognize Christ's hand in our lives, and we skip off, ready to bless the next person.

That's what I see in the mirror (or glass). I see the reflection of the person I want to be—the things I want to do. But if I don't go do what I see or feel, then the scripture says I "straightway" forget what I could have done or become.

I like to imagine the afterlife sometimes. I hope there are La-Z-Boy® we get to sit in and watch the fun moments of our lives again, set to music—our own little musical montages. There won't be commercials, and we get to hold our own remotes and pause them whenever we want. We get to pick the scenes and the days. I hope while I watch, I get to eat hot, buttered popcorn with Skittles® in it. I hope that happens.

I have had so many beautiful moments that I would love to relive. Many of those moments will include the times when my kids were small. Those days went by so fast, and sometimes I was in such a hurry to get them to bed so I could get five minutes of peace. I miss those days so much.

You parents who are still there, I know how challenging it can be. You're doing better than you know. I'm certainly not judging you for how you spend your time. I'm just saying, as a mom of teenagers and beyond, the days of snuggles and handholding are over. So if you get a chance today, hold their hands a tad longer and read them stories. Find moments to put away your phones, and don't let the beautiful dreams of fancy kitchens and perfectly organized pantries get more attention than the sweet, little people at your feet.

Because here is a fact. As I sit here imagining the scenes I would like to replay after I leave this life, not one of them included a piece of furniture I bought, a paint color on the wall, or the size of my body. Not one. These will be the least important parts of our lives when we get to the other side. Why do we care about them so much while we are here? Can you imagine saying, "Oh, rewind! Rewind! Look at those pillows on my bed. Dang it! Why won't that kid scoot over so you can see how adorable they were? It took me five months to find that perfect shade of blue."

I'm derailing again. Where are we? Oh ya, there is another place in heaven that I've imagined that I hope *doesn't* come to pass. I sure hope there isn't a room called the "Your Face in All Those Glasses" room. Because if there is, I don't want to go in there. For surely there will be so many better Melanies, so many instances I *straightway forgot*.

I don't think hell will be fire and burning. Hell will be seeing all the time we spent on dumb things and all the opportunities we missed. Hell will be that room with all those mirrors. I don't want that. So, I will pray hard every day for the strength to do what I saw in that glass.

Here's a real-life example of being a hearer but not a doer. I'll share so you can learn from my dumbness instead of being dumb yourself.

One day after reading the scriptures, I felt like I should visit a widow in my ward. I thought, *Ok, I'll make some cookies and take them over*. And then I went my way. I'm sure I was doing important things. I'm not saying that our days aren't filled with so many things to do. When kids are little, there isn't much time to do anything besides clean, feed, wash clothes, bathe, and repeat. Add a job there and be a wife or a husband, and wow, where did the time go? During that time, most of the service you give will be right inside your own walls. Don't discount that. I spent too many years beating myself up for not serving the whole world because I didn't think scurrying around to find an Abe Lincoln top hat and beard at 10 p.m. the night before wax museum day at school was serving the Lord. Cleaning up barf wasn't service in the kingdom, was it? I was wrong. It counts so much.

Don't let Satan tell you that what you're doing in your home is insignificant. It's not. We all have seasons. If your season is little kids, putting the Costco orange chicken in the oven and mustering up some rice counts as your service for the day. Calling your husband and saying you just can't do anymore and asking him to pick up Taco Bell on the way home counts as his service. There's a fantastic talk by President Dallin H. Oaks that talks about how Satan works on our strengths, not just our weaknesses. I think this importantly applies to trying to do too much outside the home when kids are small, and time is so limited.

> A willingness to sacrifice all we possess in the work of the Lord is surely a strength. In fact, it is a covenant we make in sacred places. But even this strength can bring us down if we fail to confine our sacrifices to those things the Lord and his leaders have asked of us at this time. We should say with Alma, "Why should I desire more than to perform the work to which I have been called?[31]

You can't do it all.

In the podcast, sometimes, I say things that have nothing to do with the lesson, and I wonder where it comes from. Then I will get a message or email that says that part was just what someone needed. I'm not sure why I just went on a tangent about Satan tempting women, especially women with small children, to feel bad that they aren't out taking care of the whole world. Maybe it was for you.

But be careful. That rant didn't give you permission to sit home on your phone and pin new kitchens all day and then say, "Melanie said I don't have time to serve. My kids are small." If you think that's what I said, you've missed my point. My point was that there are women out there who don't count service in the home as service. I was one of these women for a long time. I'm not saying that I was out serving the whole world all the time, not at all. But Satan got really good at making me feel bad that I wasn't OUT doing more.

Let this scripture guide your season of life. "Wherefore, be not weary in well-doing, for ye are laying the foundation of a great work. And out of small things proceedeth that which is great" (Doctrine and Covenants 64:33). Wiping noses and bottoms may be your small things right now, but you're laying the foundation of little people's lives! It counts. Let it count, parents.

Last week, one of my son's very best friends spoke in church. As this boy was finishing up his freshman year of high school, the doctors found and removed a very large brain tumor. The surgery left him unable to speak, walk, or do much of anything for himself for a long time. It has been a rough four years, and there are many things he still can't do on his own.

He shared the story of the Last Supper when the Lord was washing all the disciples' feet. When the Savior got to Peter, Peter said, "Thou shalt never wash my feet," and then, "Jesus answered him, 'If I wash thee not, thou hast no part with me.'" Peter then replied, "Lord, not my feet only, but also *my* hands and *my* head" (John 13:8). My son's friend then made the point that in order to be Christ's disciples, we also need to *receive* service. He spoke of all the hours his friends spent just sitting with him and all the hours of selfless service he was the beneficiary of. We were all weeping. The Spirit confirmed the truth of his words in such a powerful way.

I needed a ride to the airport a few months back. A friend of mine had flown into town for just three short days. We had tried to get together, but we couldn't get our schedules to align. Finally, she offered to take me to the airport so we could spend that ride chatting. I countered her offer by saying that I was not going to add a third-round trip to the airport to her extremely short visit. After some back and forth, I agreed to let her take me. During our drive, I told her I felt so guilty for taking part of her limited time. Her answer was a lesson to me. She replied, "I never feel guilty when people serve me. I love how I feel when I serve others, so why would I take that opportunity away from someone else?"

Wow.

Some of us may be in a situation where we are the ones receiving service. Satan is also good at making us feel bad when we *need* help, not just when we are not giving it the way we hope. If your season in life is depending on the help of others, then please, think of *their* faces in *their* glasses one day. Think of the joy they will feel as they remember following promptings to help you. There are so many ways to follow the Savior—yours may be letting others wash your feet for a time. Let it count.

That took me away from my story for a while. Goodness! I'm sure you don't even remember where I started. I was talking about one morning feeling the prompting to visit a widow in my ward. I didn't have time to make cookies, and for some dumb reason, we tell ourselves we have to take a treat, or we can't visit someone in need. Needless to say, days went by and then weeks. Finally, one afternoon I decided to make the cookies and take them over.

When I knocked on the door, I explained the prompting weeks earlier and presented the cookies. She looked at me and said so kindly, "I wonder what I needed that day."

Ahhhhhh! Don't end up there! Be the person who sees that face and runs and does it. Buy a bunch of Oreos® or Mint Milano® cookies at the store and put them in a drawer for emergency visits. Cut some roses from your yard or draw a heart on a piece of paper and put it in a bag and take it. Once, I wrote a scripture on paper, tied it around an avocado, and took it to a woman's house. I had no idea why I was there, but I wasn't going to let not having a treat stop me from being about Christ's business.

Satan says you're no good if you don't take a treat. Christ says, "You *are* the treat. Just go already!"

One last thing I like to add to this prayer—I'm talking about the prayer at the end of our study session, in case you forgot (wink). I like to thank Heavenly Father for the events and people in my life that led to me possessing the Book of Mormon. I vividly remember a day on my mission thanking Heavenly Father for Mormon and Moroni. I had just spent the day riding around on my bike with a gigantic backpack on my back. In it was an English set of scriptures and a Japanese set. I had flip charts and teaching videos—big ol' VHS tapes, and a bunch of other stuff. That backpack was HEAVY. I thought then about gold plates and how they were probably hard to shlep around. I was grateful for those men and their sacrifice that day.

Another time I thanked Heavenly Father for Martin Harris for mortgaging his farm for the first printing of the Book of Mormon. I've thanked heaven for the missionaries that found my first ancestors and the missionaries who continue to flood the earth with this beautiful book. I continually thank my Father in Heaven for Joseph Smith and the whole life that he devoted to bringing forth this gospel and the Book of Mormon.

Everyone seems to have their two cents about Joseph these days. As for me, I will not judge that man. I will only praise and adore him. I know how hard it is to serve in a big calling or do hard things the Lord has asked us to do. Every second of his life was full of hard things. Satan did all he could to stop every step Joseph took. I can't imagine the opposition. I can't believe all he accomplished, and I will be grateful for him every day.

If you're in a place where you've heard things about his life that you don't like and maybe your testimony is wavering, remember this. Doctrine and Covenants 64 verses 6-7 say, "There are those who have sought occasion against him [Joseph Smith] without cause; Nevertheless, he has sinned; but verily I say unto you, I, the Lord, forgive sins."

Isn't that awesome? Ya, guess what? We all sin. Stop worrying about what he may or may not have done wrong and look at all he did right. Elder Neil L. Anderson agrees with me. He said:

> To those of faith who, looking through the colored glasses of the 21st century, honestly question events or statements of the Prophet Joseph from nearly 200 years ago, may I share some friendly advice: For now, give Brother Joseph a break! In a future day, you will have 100 times more information than from all of today's search engines combined, and it will come from our all-knowing Father in Heaven. Consider the totality of Joseph's life—born in poverty and given little formal education, he translated the Book of Mormon in less than 90 days. Tens of thousands of honest, devoted men and women embraced the cause of the Restoration. At age 38, Joseph sealed his witness with his blood. I testify that Joseph Smith was a prophet of God.[32]

Elder Marcus B. Nash put it so well: "Rather than have heartburn over the fact that Joseph was a human being, I am awe-inspired by what the Lord made of him and am encouraged by it to believe that the Lord can make something even of weak me."[33]

The Lord has always chosen the weak things of the world to testify of truth. They are the ones who have to lean on God the most.

The fact that God has trusted me in all my chaos to testify of His gospel over the podcast for four years is a wonder in and of itself. I'm weak, weak, weak. But because of this, I know where I have to turn every single week. I've learned throughout my life to pray and ask Him to wrap His spirit around my inadequate words in order for those words to help someone feel His love.

I love Joseph Smith. Without him, my life would be so hard and sad. Because of him, I have this beautiful gospel and the Book of Mormon, which the Lord uses to guide me every day. I will stand in whatever long ol' line in heaven to meet that man someday. He's my hero.

Remember the promises given in the introduction of the Book of Mormon? I'll reiterate part of it here: "Those who gain this divine witness [that the Book of Mormon is the word of God] from the Holy Spirit will also come to know by the same power that Jesus Christ is the Savior of the world, that Joseph Smith is His revelator and prophet in these last days ..."[34]

That's it! Do you get it? Do you see? All the time I've spent searching, pondering, and turning to the Book of Mormon has not only led me to a testimony that the book is true but led me to love and revere the Prophet Joseph Smith. It's another two-for-one. I didn't put two and two together until just this minute. Wahoo!! Look what it did for me!

If you need to get past your bad thoughts and feelings about Joseph Smith, don't head to the internet to learn more about what he may or may not have said or done. Turn to the Book of Mormon.

Ponder the words and messages. Your mind will straighten out. Love and admiration will return.

Our dear, sweet prophet, President Russell M. Nelson, testified, "When I think of the Book of Mormon, I think of the word power. The truths of the Book of Mormon have the power to heal, comfort, restore, succor, strengthen, console, and cheer our souls."[35]

Let the healing power of the Savior of the world, found in the Book of Mormon, bring you back to the faith you had. Let Him heal your hurt and mistrust. Let Him cleanse your mind of the garbage that has taken the place of your love for the Savior and the Restoration. He can do that.

President Nelson advised, "I plead with you who have distanced yourselves from the Church and with you who have not yet really sought to know that the Savior's Church has been restored. Do the spiritual work to find out for yourselves, and please do it now. Time is running out."[36]

If you are thinking of leaving your faith behind, don't leave!

Let the power of the Savior made manifest in the Book of Mormon heal you.

If you've left and have for some miraculous reason found my book, turn to the Book of Mormon.

Let the Savior heal you.

He can, and He will.

Wow. This chapter was just supposed to be about your little prayer at the end. I guess if you didn't know what to pray about, you have plenty of ideas now.

PART 2

CHAPTER 17

"And if men come unto me I will show unto them their weakness. I give unto men weakness that they may be humble; and my grace is sufficient for all men that humble themselves before me; for if they humble themselves before me, and have faith in me, then will I make weak things become strong unto them."

Ether 12:27

I n Kyoto, my second companion and I were teaching a very sweet woman I will call Naomi. While taking the discussions, she had come to know that the church was true. She wanted to be baptized, but there was a problem. She was an avid smoker and just couldn't stop. She was trying but continually failing; she didn't know what to do.

After leaving a discussion with her one night, my companion and I had a genius idea. We bought a pack of cigarettes from a vending machine on the way home. (Ya, they even have alcohol in vending machines in Japan. If you aren't old enough to buy it, you don't. It's fantastic.)

We quickly dumped the cigarettes in the trash, and then we covered the box with some paper and a picture of Jesus on the front. Inside, we rolled up little paper-like fake cigarettes and wrote scriptures on them about avoiding temptation and doing hard things. (Thinking about it now, it probably still smelled like cigarettes. That probably wasn't the smartest thing. But after you hear what happened, you won't care that we put that temptation right back in her hand. Give us a break. We were young.)

The next time we met, we gave her our little fake pack. We told her, "Every time you want to smoke, just pull out one of these scriptures and look it up. This will help you avoid temptation." After a good pep talk and a prayer together, we left. I remember thinking this was going to work. I had faith in this book and its power.

When we got together again, we asked her how it went. She said, "Well, you know that pack you gave me? I burned through that pack in the first hour. But do you know what? Every time I wanted to smoke after that, I just opened up the Book of Mormon, and no matter where I opened it, there was something about avoiding temptation or something else that comforted me and gave me the power to resist. I have completely stopped smoking."

Elder Marcus B. Nash said:

> We can choose to be defined by our weakness, to be conquered by it, or we can choose to be motivated by it to humbly seek the Master's guidance and grace, His enabling power. This, then, is the potential virtue of weakness: if, by

our choice, weakness moves us to humble ourselves before the Savior and to exercise our
faith in Him, then by His Atonement we can
become strong.[37]

There is no quicker way to turn to the Master to
have Him help us conquer our weaknesses than by
turning to the Book of Mormon.

I witnessed Christ's power, felt through the pages
of the Book of Mormon, free Naomi from an addiction she was helpless to break on her own. It trans-
formed her. It gave her the ability to do something
she couldn't do on her own.

Right before I started the podcast in January
2019, I was having a rough time near the end of my
divorce proceedings. I went to my brother-in-law and
asked for a blessing. Many miraculous things were
said in that blessing that have guided me through
these past few years. One thing he said was, "The
Book of Mormon will heal you physically as well as
mentally." It was something I had never thought of,
and I wasn't sure I understood what the Lord was
saying. As I ponder the story of Naomi and another
story I am about to tell you, I think I understand
what he meant.

The power of Christ is made available to us in its
very purest form in the Book of Mormon. Here, we
are best able to hear His voice. We can feel His love
and obtain His sanctifying and cleansing power. Most
of the time, this is a spiritual matter. But sometimes,
like in these stories, the power of Christ felt through
the pages of the Book of Mormon also heals us phys-

ically. We are given the power to overcome addiction and change. It's a miracle.

One of my best friends in the entire world is a woman named Emily. I met her in Virginia over a quarter century ago. (Is that right? Sheesh! We are old.) We met when our husbands were in school. We tended each other's fussy babies and served in really hard callings together. We had zero dollars, and we didn't care at all. We'd load our kids up in my cool, old green Dodge Caravan and take them to the park or to the free play time at the mall. We planned on marrying our kids off to each other when they were old, and we were always laughing. I'm so grateful that we still keep in touch. I love her so much.

If anyone is my gospel twin, it's her. Whenever we talk, it takes about three minutes to get past what's going on in our lives and straight to some aspect of the gospel. I love talking about all things spiritual with her. She's so wise.

Through her, I met her sister Lizzy. I had the beautiful opportunity to interview her a few years back about her experience with postpartum depression, opioid addiction, and the power of redemption. I want to share a small part of Lizzy's story, with her permission.

Lizzy was an overachiever who had always succeeded in life. She got good grades, was involved in many sports and extracurricular activities, had many jobs, and worked hard. She always strived to be the best at everything she did. She worked full-time while going to college and got a nursing degree. And while this was awesome, and she excelled at so many things, her world fell apart when she came to something she couldn't control or master.

When she and her husband wanted to get pregnant, it didn't happen right away. After a year of trying, they decided on infertility treatment, which didn't initially work. Three years later, she was finally blessed with the child she had wanted so badly. She was going to be the best mother—right? Because she strove for perfection in all she did. But she hadn't expected postpartum depression and the struggles that ensued.

She didn't want to tell anyone how she felt, because that would be admitting failure—and Lizzy didn't fail! How hypocritical would it be to admit she wasn't feeling happy when this baby was all she had hoped and prayed for, for over four years! (*Here is a link to my interview with Lizzy and her husband and some valuable resources to help you if you aren't feeling right after having a baby. It's ok to feel terrible! It happens so often. Please, tell someone how you are feeling. http://comefollowmeforus.com/s2episode15/)

About three weeks after her baby was born, she felt a lot of anxiety and worry. One day, she got a terrible headache. She had some narcotics she had received after having the baby that she hadn't used. When she took it, not only did the headache go away, but she felt good. Really good. She felt like everything was going to be ok. She made phone calls she hadn't been able to make, went on a walk, and cleaned her house. As she continued to take the pills, the old, super-capable Lizzy was back.

She recalls the following:

> During the early parts of my recovery, I felt extremely betrayed by God. I didn't have a relationship with my Savior, Jesus Christ, and I felt like there was not an ounce of hope in this world for me. My feelings of resentment toward Heavenly Father were all based around the fact that I was literally fulfilling my divine nature of "multiplying and replenishing the earth." Not to mention at the time, I was serving faithfully in the Young Women's presidency. Shortly after the birth of my daughter, I was diagnosed with postpartum depression, anxiety, and psychosis. I truly wondered why this would happen to me because leading up to this point in my life, I had done nothing but stay on the covenant path.

She decided she would "just utilize opiates until all my hormones balanced out and I could return to my normal self. Fast forward, I was addicted and using them daily; I couldn't function without them." She initially got more from her OB and then her regular doctor, but eventually, she ran out.

She started to steal from family and friends' medicine cabinets. Eventually, she was confronted, and to make everyone happy, she participated in outpatient rehab. She was clean for about ninety days.

But then she returned to being a nurse, and the floodgates opened wide. She was able to get her hands on drugs again, and within a month and a half, she was arrested for writing her own prescriptions. She went to jail for six days.

She says that the first night there in jail, she was overcome with darkness. The palpability of Satan's influence in that prison was so strong. On the second day, she decided that she would never be able to change; it was just too hard. She then made a plan to take her life when she returned home. She was so far from the perfect person she was supposed to be. She knew she could never get back there.

Luckily, when she got out, she couldn't go home, where the tools for the planned suicide were readily available. She went to her parents' house. It was here that she got two essential phone calls and some advice that changed her life. Her brother called her and told her that he loved her. Then, while talking to her brother, her grandmother called and told her the same thing. So many people had distanced themselves from her at this point. She understood the hurt she had caused and knew they had to protect themselves and their families. Many of them had been through this before with other family members, and those other family members hadn't gotten better. She understood that distance was necessary for many around her.

Feeling very alone and unworthy of love, these two almost simultaneous declarations of compassion began to crack the shell of despair she had wrapped around herself. Her brother began to give her some advice. She didn't want advice, and she didn't want to listen to him. But the word *love* kept coming back to her mind. "He loves me. He's offering this out of love." She decided to listen.

I told him how hopeless I felt and what a failure I was—not just as a mom, but as a human! I told him that I didn't think I could do it. Despite all the professional help, I still felt shame on a level that felt too far to come back from.

He recommended that I read the Book of Mormon cover to cover. At first, I scoffed at the advice, telling him that I hadn't prayed in so long. I barely remembered what the Spirit felt like, and I thought reading the Book of Mormon would be a waste. My brother recommended that I read it and highlight any part that acknowledged mercy, justice, or grace.

I didn't follow the storyline. I didn't look up words I didn't know. I just stuck to my sole purpose of reading it for the pure intent of what the healing and cleansing power of the atonement can do, especially what it can do for me. He said he thought that I wasn't allowing myself to accept the Atonement because he didn't think I understood it. He was definitely right; I felt the crushing weight of Satan's grasp at a level that was beyond anything redeemable or forgivable.

I decided to take his advice—nothing up to this point was working, and I was at the end of my rope. I prayed a simple prayer, prior to starting, that I would be able to understand the Atonement. Even if I wasn't sure it would work for me, I wanted to try to understand better what the Savior did for me.

She said the moment she opened the Book of Mormon, she felt light and love flood back into her life. Going back to her words, she testified:

> The end result was incredible, awe-inspiring, and truly life-saving. It wasn't the stories of prophets of old in the Book of Mormon that changed my life. It was the powerful prophesying of Jesus Christ. I learned that the Atonement is all-encompassing! The Savior pulled me out of the depths of suicidal ideation and total hopelessness. I felt the Atonement working for me in the first part of recovery when I wasn't going to church and didn't feel worthy of receiving forgiveness. The Atonement was there for me even when I was mad at Heavenly Father.
>
> I grew up believing that my worth was based on choices I made, and that forgiveness was deemed for those who were living their lives perfectly. What I learned from the Book of Mormon is that Jesus Christ's love is for everyone despite their mistakes. He can love through imperfections because He understands them to the greatest extent. The bottom line is that the Atonement works for any and all situations. It works for any emotion, feeling, or behavior. The Atonement of my Savior Jesus Christ worked and works so perfectly for me.

One of the most humbling discoveries I made about myself during this time is that Heavenly Father and Jesus Christ are always there, even if I am mad or unwilling to acknowledge this truth. I decided before reading the Book of Mormon that I would be open and willing because my brother read Moroni Chapter 10, verse 4 to me. It tells us to ask God if the things in the book are true with a SINCERE heart and real intent. I often wonder if my experience and life in the gospel and in general would be different had I been prideful or disingenuous. But because I sincerely wanted to understand the power of Jesus Christ, the Holy Ghost spoke the truth plain as day to me. I am more than grateful for the Book of Mormon and how it truly changed not only my life but my heart.

Elder Bednar said, "This mighty change is not simply the result of working harder or developing greater individual discipline. Rather it is the consequence of a fundamental change of our desires, our motives, and our natures made possible through the Atonement of Christ the Lord."[38]

I told Lizzy she needs to write a book about her experience. I hope she does. There is so much more to her story—the person she became, the dependence on the Lord that she developed. She doesn't just hog all that love she feels from the Savior to herself. As she has grown closer to Jesus, she has developed a desire to treat others better and to serve more.

She extends forgiveness to others more easily. The list goes on and on. She currently works with people dealing with addictions. Christ changed her whole life—and it started in the Book of Mormon.

Her story is a miracle. We all one day will need our own miracles. If we can just remember where to turn at that time, we will be ok. Trust her story. Believe in the power that changed her life. Turn to the Book of Mormon and the Savior.

I have another compelling story of a missionary blessed by the power of the Book of Mormon. I'll call her Sister Jordan. She told me about a pornography addiction she had before she left on her mission and how she thought it would be okay because she was going to be a missionary. As a full-time representative of Jesus Christ, surely the temptation would be gone. Right? But months in, it wasn't gone. In fact, she felt the temptation and struggle amplify. She couldn't get those images out of her mind. She felt she couldn't be a good missionary with all of that whirling around in her head. Finally, she decided she needed to go home.

Sister Jordan told her mission president what was going on and that she felt it would be best to return home. Her mission president disagreed. He suggested that she return to their apartment and make studying the Book of Mormon daily her number one priority. Her mission president assured her that she would be ok and would be able to finish her mission.

With tears running down her face, this missionary said to me, "The Book of Mormon mended my mind!" She bore powerful testimony that those images were taken out of her head and did not return. She testified about feeling the Savior's power as she immersed herself in the pages of this beautiful book.

Naomi stopped smoking. Lizzy didn't take her life, felt hope, and was able to change her course completely. Sister Jordan's mind was cleansed of the unwanted images that had once dominated her thoughts. She finished a full and successful mission.

President Nelson testified:

> The Book of Mormon provides the fullest and most authoritative understanding of the Atonement of Jesus Christ to be found anywhere. It teaches what it really means to be born again ... The full power of the gospel of Jesus Christ is contained in the Book of Mormon. Period.[39]

How is this so?

Because Christ is the Word! He is there. He is waiting for us to open it up and find Him. He wants us to hear His voice, become His sheep, and follow Him.

President Nelson continued, "When I think of the Book of Mormon, I think of the word power. The truths of the Book of Mormon have the power to heal, comfort, restore, succor, strengthen, console, and cheer our souls."[40]

What are your burdens? What do you need help changing? Bring those things to the Lord. Pray. Ask for help and then trust, be sincere. Believe that Christ is there and can bring about these same kinds of miracles in your own life.

Elder David E. Bednar taught:

> May I suggest that the Book of Mormon is our
> handbook of instructions as we travel the path-
> way ... to have our hearts changed.

> I suspect that you and I are much more familiar
> with the nature of the redeeming power of the
> Atonement than we are with the enabling power
> of the Atonement. It is one thing to know that
> Jesus Christ came to earth to die for us. That is
> fundamental and foundational to the doctrine of
> Christ. But we also need to appreciate that the
> Lord desires, through His Atonement and by
> the power of the Holy Ghost, to live in us—not
> only to direct us but also to empower us.[41]

Isn't that beautiful? Christ wants to live in us.
Elder Bednar continued:

> I frankly do not think many of us "get it" con-
> cerning this enabling and strengthening aspect
> of the Atonement, and I wonder if we mistaken-
> ly believe we must make the journey from good
> to better and become a saint all by ourselves
> through sheer grit, willpower, and discipline,
> and with our obviously limited capacities.[42]

I think I grew up partly believing that to be true.
I lived in a time when I often heard about Christ
making up some gap at the end of our lives. I mis-

takenly thought that I had to do my best to perfect myself, and after all my hard work, that thing He did for me in that garden that day would fix what wasn't completely fixable on my own. But I was so wrong. What I've learned from the Book of Mormon, especially from a story in Mosiah 24, is that Christ is with us the whole time!! He isn't just going to show up at the end and mediate for us in front of God. He has the ability to be with us the whole time. Right now. He enables us with power to overcome addiction and weakness. He provides the needed power to change.

The Savior has already suffered for EVERY-THING. Physical, emotional, sin, all of it. He is trying to achieve a relationship with us through repentance. Repentance isn't us atoning or paying for anything—it is turning back to Him and seeing Him more clearly so we can love Him better for what HE HAS ALREADY DONE.

I had a friend who told me about her "faith crisis." She had read things that had happened in church history that she didn't like. She'd come across a lot of conflicting information and was having a hard time discerning what of it was true. She felt that somehow prophets should be more perfect than the rest of us. She thought they should have all been above making mistakes. She'd also had experiences in life where she felt God had let her down, and her faith was dwindling; in fact, it was almost extinguished.

It was at this time that she ran into a family friend at a party who happened to be the pastor for another religion. As they spoke, she began to disclose to him some of her concerns. She expressed her doubts and told him she was ready to leave it all behind. He gave her some advice that changed her trajectory. It was advice so similar to the advice Lizzy's brother gave her that pivotal day.

He said, "Before you leave all the faith you've had, please take some time and study *grace*." Like Lizzy, she was challenged to learn more fully what the Savior was offering her. She told me that she spent the next year searching for and reading everything she could get her hands on about grace. Through the pages of the Bible, the Book of Mormon, and the words of the apostles and prophets, she came to better understand our dear Savior and all He offers us. She grew to love the Savior. She testified that as she better understood and felt all the grace, love, and forgiveness He was offering her, she was then able to extend that forgiveness and grace to others, including imperfect prophets and people of the past.

Alma the younger tells us about his father's conversion in the Book of Mormon. He said of his father's experience:

> And according to his faith there was a mighty change wrought in his heart. Behold I say unto you that this is all true. And behold, he preached the word unto your fathers, and a mighty change was also wrought in their hearts, and they humbled themselves and put their trust in the true and living God. And behold, they were faithful until the end; therefore they were saved.

"And now behold, I ask of you ...have ye spiritually been born of God? Have ye received his image in your countenances? Have ye experienced this mighty change in your hearts?" (Alma 5:12, 14).

If you haven't, it's not too late. Let the word work in you. Search grace. Read about Jesus. Turn to the Book of Mormon. You will find Him there again and again.

Elder Benjamin Tai said,

Jesus Christ is the Master Physician. Through His Atonement, He binds up our wounds, takes upon Himself our infirmities, and heals our broken hearts. Through His grace our weakness can become strong. He invites us to follow Him by learning of Him, listening to His words, and walking in the meekness of His Spirit. He has promised to help us in this lifelong process of conversion, which transforms us and brings everlasting joy. The Savior has given us the Book of Mormon as a powerful tool to aid in conversion.[43]

CHAPTER 18

*"...blessed are you because of your faith
in my work..."*

Doctrine and Covenants 31:1-2

After my first husband left the church, his return became the primary purpose for our fast every month. The kids and I would fast and pray that Dad would change his mind, have some great experience, or somehow decide that he wanted to come back.

After months, my kids began to lose faith in the process; it wasn't working. I too began to lose hope that we would see a change anytime soon.

The following fast Sunday, I decided to fast for my children. Yes, Dad was out for the moment, but please, Heavenly Father, protect my children's testimonies. Please help them stay strong despite differing opinions and the different dynamics that are now in our home.

I can't remember for sure if it was the next day or two days later, but I just opened my scriptures that day to read. It wasn't right where I had been reading and I didn't start in the topical guide. I just opened my scriptures and started reading.

I was in Doctrine and Covenants 31. Here, the Lord is giving Thomas Marsh some counsel. In verse one, it says, "Thomas, my son."

I forgot to mention that my mission president suggested we put our name in place of the person we are reading about. This is kind of nice because it tailors the message to you. I have had some very sweet experiences as I have applied this principle. It's not so sweet when you get compared to murmuring Laman, or a blood-thirsty Ammoron, the king of the Lamanites. But who knows, maybe you'll need it the day you read about Ammaron and his hatred, grudge-holding, and complaining about all the wrongs that happened to his ancestors. Perhaps that will be the weekend you need to go to your Uncle Lou's funeral, and you've been grumbling, "I would rather be *in that coffin* than see that side of the family. They are nuts. Do you remember what his wife said to Mom in 1978?" Maybe by placing your name there, you will see what can happen when you don't forgive. You hear the voice of the Lord whisper, "It's time to let it go."

Or who knows, maybe you'll say, "Man, Uncle Lou was just like Ammoron. He caused trouble all the time! I hate that guy." Or maybe reading Moroni's plan to trick the Lamanites with strong wine reminds you that Lou is just a drunk, and maybe you should finally forgive him. I don't know what you will let the Spirit teach you that day. I don't know that your mom's side of the family is the worst. Who's Uncle Lou? What is happening? All I'm saying is if you turn to Him every day by opening the scriptures, you will hear what you need to hear.

Back to my story and putting *my* name in it. I replaced 'Thomas, my son,' with Melanie.

> [Melanie, my daughter,] blessed are you because of your faith in my work. Behold, you have had many afflictions because of your family; nevertheless, I will bless you and your family, yea, your little ones; and the day cometh that they will believe and know the truth and be one with you in my church (Doctrine and Covenants 31:1-2).

Can you believe it? Do you believe me now when I say Christ knows where all the words are? That couldn't have been a coincidence. There's just no way. Sometimes the answers are freaky specific, like this one. Other times the scriptures we read just elicit feelings in us—feelings like comfort or peace. Either way, the Lord can and does communicate with us. It's such a big deal.

This experience wasn't just a big deal to me on November 25, 2011. It's a big deal to me now. Because now, four out of five of my children no longer believe or go to church with me. That would be pretty depressing if it weren't for this experience. But I trust the Lord. I trust the things He tells me, especially when it comes as I search the scriptures and feel the whoosh of the Spirit tell me that this answer is from God. He promised me that day that all my kids would be back. So, while I continue to pray for them and try to lead and guide them the best I can, my soul isn't wracked in torment over this thing. I know that God has a plan for them and me. Some of these blessings may not even happen until the other side, but I can rest easy until then. As long as I keep the commandments and try my best to live up to my covenants, God will help this come to pass.

I know it because God doesn't lie.

CHAPTER 19

*"And I will bless her with blessings, and multiply
a multiplicity of blessings upon her, and upon
her generations forever and ever."*

Doctrine and Covenants 97:28

After it was decided that my first husband and I were going to divorce, I started thinking about where I was going to live. Our current home was too big and would be too expensive for me to maintain. The weeks when my kids weren't there were brutal. All those empty rooms made me sad. It felt like that 1990's blockbuster hit, *Home Alone*, when Kevin gets left behind and wanders in and out of empty rooms, and then mistakenly thinks that he made his family disappear. Except, in my house and my story, I didn't then smile, raise my eyebrows up and down, and then go jump on all the beds and run laughing around the dining room table, and up and down the stairs. I would actually cry for hours after my children left every week. I had been a full-time mom to five children for over twenty years, and all of a sudden, I was home alone.

But this story isn't about boo-hoo sadness—it's about finding a new place to live. And don't worry; eventually, I jumped on the beds while eating bags of popcorn and lit fireworks in a bucket, pretending to be a mob boss to scare burglars away.

That's not true. I just forgot I loved that movie and got carried away. I should go watch it.

What *did* happen during that time was I went over to some homes being built near mine, and I found this model home that I loved. It was beautiful! It was a good downsize, just one story, and only had one big family room and kitchen area. There weren't any extra rooms to clean, and without a formal dining and living room, I would need far less furniture, etc. It was awesome.

I immediately fell in love with the idea of building this house by myself. Now don't be crazy. I wasn't actually going to grab a hammer and some nails and start throwing up two-by-fours. Nor was I designing a house from scratch. But I would be able to go to a design center and pick my cabinets and flooring, etc. I had never done that before, and it sounded like a happy distraction.

But I had to pop that daydream bubble before I got carried away. I thought, *This is absurd! How am I going to buy a house now? The divorce isn't settled yet. I don't have any income or anything. Knock this ridiculousness off.*

I couldn't stop thinking about it though, and I couldn't quit going over there. It felt like it would be a lovely, fresh start. But I would have to wait and see what happened in the divorce. We had just begun the proceedings, and it looked like it would be a while

until we got it all hammered out. I would probably have to rent for a time and then go from there.

I started praying. "Where should I live? What
should I do? Do I build a house? Do I try to stay
here in this big, expensive house?" Day in and day
out, all I could think about was building that house.

I thought, *This can't be my answer! Of course, I want
that house! It's a brand-new house. It's so nice. It's not my
answer. It can't be.* The builder only had a few lots left,
so if I was going to even try to get the house, I had
to make a quick decision. To make matters worse,
I was getting ready to head out of town on a trip.
I literally had only a few days to figure out what
I was going to do.

So, I went to the temple. When I really need answers in my life, I head to the Book of Mormon and
to the temple. Do you want to know a cool life hack?
Read the scriptures IN THE TEMPLE. It's a killer
combo! But that day, the whole time I was in a temple, I kept thinking, *Build that house. Build that house.*
But I couldn't accept it could be the answer. *You're being a spoiled little girl who wants a brand-new house. That's
all.* No other ideas came to my mind, but I couldn't
feel at peace about it. I left the temple even more
confused than I was when I got there.

Driving back, I decided to put the house hunt
on the back burner and started thinking about some
very specific feelings I had in the temple about sacrifice. I decided to look up some scriptures about
sacrifice and see if there were any that could clarify
what I was feeling.

After the temple, I was meeting some friends for
lunch. I got there a little early, and while waiting for

others to show up, I opened up my phone and looked up "sacrifice" in the topical guide, on the church app. There was a cornucopia of scriptures about sacrifice—156 to be exact. Now, remember what I've said, God knows where all the words are. I think it's easy for Him to direct us to what He needs to tell us.

I clicked on the very first one that I thought might give me clarity. It was Doctrine and Covenants Section 97. Starting in verse eight, it says:

> Verily I say unto you, all among them who know their hearts are honest, and are broken, and their spirits contrite, and are willing to observe their covenants by sacrifice—yea, every sacrifice which I, the Lord, shall command—they are accepted of me.

I felt the sweet movings of the Spirit. I felt Heavenly Father saying, "You've made a lot of sacrifices the past few years because of your faith. I know it hasn't been easy. I see you. Thanks for trying so hard. Thanks for relying on your covenants."

I continued to read. In verse ten, I stopped. I couldn't believe what I read.

It said, "Verily I say unto you, that it is my will that a house should be built ..." And the next verse was the kicker. "Yea, let it be built speedily."

The Red Sea split for me in that Chili's® parking lot. The whoosh of the Spirit filled my car. Could I have read anything more specific to my situation? I hadn't looked up "build + house" in the topical guide. If so, I would have second-guessed the experience. But I hadn't. I had looked up *sacrifice*. I was thinking of something totally different.

I had about three days to decide whether I could put money down to start building the house or not. I couldn't deny the answer I had been given in my car. I went back to the builder and said, "I want to build this house." And they said, "Okay, well, no one's gonna loan you any money. You don't even know how much money you're gonna have from your divorce. You don't have a job yet. You don't know much of anything." I thought to myself, *I know what the Lord wants me to do.* I moved forward.

The first lender we reached out to put their hand on their belly and, with a hearty laugh, said, "Ha ha ha! No way."

The next lender said, with even more conviction, "Are you kidding? No way. We won't lend you a dime." Had I not read that Scripture and felt the overwhelming confirmation of the Holy Ghost, I would have stopped right there. It was beginning to be quite embarrassing. But the Lord said to build the house, and I knew it was the path I was supposed to take.

Long story short, the builder and I searched until we found a lender that said, "Okay, we'll do it."

I put the money down that they needed to get started, picked a lot, and left for vacation. I finally felt at peace. I didn't know how it was all going to work out, but I had faith. I'd felt the whoosh.

There were hurdles along the way. Two days before close, the lender changed their mind. I almost didn't get it. But in the end, it worked out. I got the house.

There was a girl, Karalee, who lived in that new neighborhood and had lived in my current ward for a little while. I didn't know her well, but I called her and asked her how she liked the ward and the neighborhood, etc. Quickly we became friends. I want to say she was born around 1988. To give some perspective, I graduated from high school in 1990! I'm like this old lady to her, right? But it didn't matter to her. She had four young kids, and they were adorable and fun. Don't forget, all of a sudden, I didn't have my kids every other week and was really lonely. So lonely.

Guess what happened? This sweet, young family adopted me. At the beginning of the week, when I didn't have my kids, Karalee would send me a text that said, "We're eating dinner at five o'clock on Monday, six o'clock on Tuesday, and three o'clock on Wednesday (or whatever her schedule was). There's a place set for you every night."

Although I did not take her up on her offer very often, there were a few times when I thought, *I'm not gonna sit here and be sad and lonely anymore*. I would go over to her house and eat with her family. One night we had pizza, and afterward, I went over and watched their football practices. Another night, I even sat down and told her kids a story my grandma used to tell us about little billy goats who get eaten by a wolf while their mom is gone. When it was over, they just sat there, terrified. Are we not supposed to talk about wolves tricking little kids and then eating them whole? Was it over the top? No one told my grandma that. I didn't know it was a scary story. I'm sorry if I traumatized them. Who knew?

We ate snow cones on her back porch and swam in her pool. I went to her kids' birthday parties and that first Halloween, when I had no kids to take out, I was invited over and sat in her driveway and handed out candy with her. Her sweet, little girl sat on my lap and helped pass candy out.

That same little girl has saved a place for me by her at church these last three years. Every time I'm there alone, I have people to sit with. Every week, this little girl has drawn a picture of me and her; complete with the outfits we are wearing that day. Those pictures are my treasures, and that sweet family carried me through the roughest year of my life.

They are moving soon, and I can't even think about it. But now that I'm settled and on the other side of all those hard times, I guess it's my turn to adopt someone in need. It's my turn to save a place for someone who feels lonely.

There were others in that ward that helped me along the way and helped me make critical decisions that led to the start of the podcast. I was called to be the Young Women's president shortly after moving into the ward. I didn't know any of the girls or their families, but those sweet girls welcomed this stranger with open arms. We laughed and bore testimony together. That move was orchestrated by my Heavenly Father. I see it so clearly now. I was even told when I got set apart for that calling in the blessing from the bishop that "Heavenly Father was extremely excited for what is about to come."

If I wouldn't have gone forward to build the house, I wouldn't have talked to Karalee, and we wouldn't have become friends. I wouldn't have met those pivotal people. Building the house was also a nice distraction. When I was really sad, I would scour Pinterest looking at different cupboards and doorknobs. I occupied some of that lonely space with carpet samples and paint swatches. It kept my mind off of my broken heart during a hard period of my life.

I've thought about this situation many times. In the beginning, I couldn't wait to see what the Lord was scheming. *Was my future husband going to move in next door? Would someone in this new ward have a single brother who was fantastic, charming, and searching for a mildly hilarious, slightly chubby, silly podcast host with five kids? Why was it so important that the Lord sent me the answer in such a specific way?*

I now know without a doubt that I needed Karalee and her family. They changed my life and brought so much light to me in a dark time. I needed those people in the ward to help turn my idea of making a podcast into a reality. Maybe I needed the distraction, and maybe there was a little part of it all where the Lord just wanted to give me a sweet prize for staying faithful for so many years when it was really hard.

At the end of Doctrine and Covenants 97, that section that told me to build the house, it says, "And I will bless her with blessings, and multiply a multiplicity of blessings upon her, and upon her generations forever and ever" (Doctrine and Covenants 97:28). I don't know about all my generations yet. That will be hundreds of years in the making. But I know this now—He has not forgotten me. He has not left me comfortless. He has blessed me with amazing kids who make me proud every day. He's blessed me with a second chance at love and a husband who is good to his core. The Lord is multiplying a multiplicity of blessings for me every day. He is so good.

CHAPTER 20

*"Awake and arouse your faculties, even to an
experiment upon my words."*

Alma 32:27

I 've told you all the things I love about the Book
of Mormon. I've shared not only examples from
my life, but examples from the lives of others. Now
it's up to you. What are you going to do with this
information? The apostle James said something that
I think is so relevant. He said, "... faith, if it hath
not works is dead, being alone" (James 2:17). You
may think everything I've told you thus far is pretty
cool. You may agree with the things I have said and
have perhaps even felt the Spirit confirm truth to you
as you've read. But if you don't move forward and *do
the work* yourself, you're not going to gain a testimony
of it. James declared, "... I will shew thee my faith
by my works" (James 2:18). You need to *try* it.

It's like the face in a glass I was talking about.
You see yourself like Lizzy or that missionary or even
me. You want to believe the Lord can speak to you,
as well through the pages of this holy book. But you

may not be sure it will work *for you*. Maybe you're thinking Heavenly Father and the Savior won't want to talk *to you*. That's ok. It's a lot to take in. I just basically told you that the heavens are not closed, and that you can have a personal relationship with the Savior of the world. It makes sense that you might have some doubts, but you can do this. You need to try an experiment.

Let's approach this as a scientist would.

The most common way that scientists approach a question or concern is to use the scientific method. Most kids learn about it in third or fourth grade. So much of what we do in this life revolves around this formula.

This method, in its simplest form, contains these basic steps.

1. Ask a question.
2. Form a hypothesis—(which is essentially if/then statements that can be tested).
3. Make a prediction based on your hypothesis.
4. Test the prediction.
5. Gather data.
6. Repeat.

I like words like data and evidence. They are things that can be gathered and calculated. I've often been mocked and criticized by people who say I'm not smart because I have faith in the Gospel of Jesus Christ. People who have left my faith repeatedly rehearse to me phrases like, "You just want to stick your head in the sand." "You just follow like a sheep." "You don't use your mind." I often feel that people think I am just some spacey person flitting around after unicorns and fairies, and that I'm not intelligent because I believe in God. How often I've heard people tell me, "Religion is just a crutch for weak people."

It simply is not true. What is true is that over my almost fifty years on this planet, I have questioned, made hypotheses, and gathered data. Over and over, I have used this method as I have prayed and turned to the word of God. My data has stacked up to the point that I cannot deny the results. When you collect enough data that supports your hypothesis and validates your experiments, you come to a point where you can regard something as truth.

Some people mistakenly think that science and religion cannot exist together. On the contrary, approaching faith with the scientific method is very helpful and effective.

Hypothesis:

Heavenly Father and Jesus Christ can communicate with us through the pages of the Book of Mormon.

I have tested this statement repeatedly, and my data in the affirmative are staggering.

Alma 32 in the Book of Mormon is actually one big experiment. Alma encourages us to use the steps above to determine if the Book of Mormon is truly from God. He encourages us to experiment *with the word* of God. It's so great. I love it when science and religion hold hands and get along. They aren't at odds. God uses science all the time because He created science.

In this chapter, Alma's heart is troubled. He had just finished dealing with Korihor and all his lies and persuasions. Then he found out that another group of people had been perverting the truth and perse-cuting another set of believers in a nearby city. He needed to go try and help.

> And now, as the preaching of the word had a great tendency to lead the people to do that which was just—yea, it had had a more pow-erful effect upon the minds of the people than the sword, or anything else, which had hap-pened unto them—therefore Alma thought it was expedient that they should try the virtue of the word of God (Alma 31:5).

To know this, Alma had to have been conducting some experiments of his own. He had also been privy to other data gathered and tested by other proph-ets before him. He read the accounts of the people before him and understood the power of the word.

Ammon chopped off the arms of "not a few" La-manites that came against him and the king's ser-vants (Alma 17:34). But it wasn't until Ammon shared the word of God with the king, actually opened and read the scriptures to him, that the king's heart was changed. Alma had seen again and again that it was the Holy Ghost *confirming the words of Christ* that changed hearts and healed relationships. Alma knew that the words of Christ were vital. He decided to go try it out with the Zoromites.

You may remember this story. These were the guys that built the tower and climbed up once a week and said, "Holy Holy God, we know we are so great, and those poor chumps in town with the ratty clothes are the worst, and we know You love us best! Oh, and You're a spirit, and there will never be a Jesus. Amen." And then they climbed down and never thought about God again until the following Sunday when they did the same thing.

I love chapter 31 when it describes Alma and his brethren the first time they saw this. It says, "They were astonished beyond all measure" (Alma 31:19). Basically, they were thinking, *What in the world?* It really was so strange.

But this tower and the "we are so great, and not you" situation caused the lower class of people who weren't allowed to worship on that tower to feel sad. They believed the hype. "We can't go up the tower; therefore, we are scum, and God doesn't love us." Or something like that.

Why? Because the rich people in their fancy clothes told them that?

I guess.

Speaking of *guess*, it goes back to my story at the beginning. Sometimes wealthy people in fancy clothes make people with less feel *less* than others. That stinks. It really does. But in my case, and the Zoromites' case, that sadness was preparatory to feeling God's love.

When Alma saw how sad they were, it says he got happy. "... he beheld with great joy; for he beheld that their afflictions had truly humbled them, and that they were in a preparation to hear the word" (Alma 32:6).

We understand that they were poor in heart because they didn't have the stuff and the nice clothes and weren't invited to the tower power parties. The times that our circumstances humble us are often when we are more apt to turn to God. We *need* Him.

Alma then said, "I'm so glad that things have been so sucky for you because now you are ready to listen. The timing is fantastic. You are prepared for my experiment."

He gave them one more, little nugget of wisdom before explaining the experiment to them. He said, "because ye were compelled to be humble ye were blessed, do ye not suppose that they are more blessed who truly humble themselves because of the word?" (Alma 32:14).

Because of the word.

You will be more blessed if you let the word of God change your heart. This is so important because Alma probably saw this down the road. He knew that when things got easier, or if they hit the jackpot and could get the clothes or the pass to the tower, they might forget about God again. He wanted to teach them how to let the word of God continually govern their change.

In the following few verses, Alma reminded the people that seeking signs in order to believe doesn't work either. "Trust me, guys. I recently spent some time with this guy, Korihor ... and we all learned pretty quickly from his situation that seeking for signs isn't the answer."

Speaking of signs, I started this book with the story of Elijah and the fire lighting up the soaked altar. All the people were chanting, "The Lord is God!!" Right? But in the very next chapter, *the very next chapter*, Elijah is sitting under a tree, super discouraged.

He says, "I, even I only, am left; and they seek my life, to take it away" (1 Kings 19:10).

Wait, what? It hadn't been that long. And no one believed anymore? What the heck?

Hadn't God just shown the people who God was in a powerful way when He lit that altar? They couldn't deny it, and all of them fell on their faces *that day* and proclaimed that they knew the truth. But apparently, in the next days and weeks, they forgot the miracle and went on their way.

How was that possible? How could they forget something like that?

Because the people believed *because* of the miracle. The people were awed by pyrotechnics but didn't turn back to let the Spirit speak to their souls in a more personal way. We may see a big miracle every now and again. It may bolster our faith for a while, but it won't last. God taught Elijah a powerful lesson in the very next verse. Elijah was admonished to:

> Go forth, and stand upon the mount before the Lord. And, behold, the Lord passed by, and a great and strong wind rent the mountains, and brake in pieces the rocks before the Lord; but the Lord was not in the wind: and after the wind an earthquake; but the Lord was not in the earthquake: And after the earthquake a fire; but the Lord was not in the fire: and after the fire a still small voice (1 Kings 19:11-12).

Seeing or being part of a miracle may only change us for a minute. For true conversion, we need to learn to let the words of Jesus Christ touch our hearts on a continual basis. If you're riding on the tails of your grandma getting healed or hearing a song on the radio that told you to stay in the church after you prayed, watch out. It's not going to be enough to hold you. You have to return and listen for that *still, small voice* again and again. You have to stop asking for the earthquake and the fire to prove that God is real and the church is true, and search for that still, small voice.

Because it's that voice, Christ's voice, that will lead you home. It's what will secure your testimony. It's the voice that "notwithstanding it being a small voice it did pierce them that did hear to the center, insomuch that there was no part of their frame that it did not cause to quake; yea, it did pierce them to the very soul and did cause their hearts to burn" (3 Nephi 11:3). Hearing that voice is the bigger miracle—it's available to all of us.

Back to Alma's experiment. After he told the people that seeking signs isn't the way to know the truth, he returned to the power of the word of God and told them that it all starts with hope.

He tried to help them understand what faith is. "...faith is not to have a perfect knowledge of things; therefore if ye have faith ye hope for things which are not seen, which are true" (Alma 32:21).

If you think of faith as *hoping for things* you can't see, it is easier to realize that you have at least a particle of faith. You do.

"I hope God is real."

"I hope I will see my loved one again."

"I hope God can answer my prayers through the pages of the Book of Mormon."

See? Having hope doesn't take a whole lot of work. If you don't hope to know the gospel is true, and if you don't hope to get answers to your prayers or develop a relationship with Christ, it isn't going to work. If your sole purpose in reading this book or reading the Book of Mormon is to prove all I'm saying isn't true, Christ certainly will not manifest Himself unto you. He wants you to want it. God isn't in the business of forcing people to believe, and most times, He doesn't show Himself to us until *after* we show some faith.

Alma then told the people, "God is merciful unto all who believe on his name" (Alma 32:22). Maybe if you're having a hard time believing the Book of Mormon is the word of God, first believe in Christ. *Hope* that Christ is real. Another prophet, named Nephi, gave us a cool life hack, and *I love hacks.*

He encouraged us to "... believe in Christ; and if ye believe not in these words believe in Christ. And if ye shall believe in Christ ye will believe in these words, for they are the words of Christ, and he hath given them unto me; and they teach all men that they should do good" (2 Nephi 33:10).

Believe in Jesus. Hope that Jesus is who we think He is. That's a pretty good starting place to begin this experiment.

CHAPTER 21

"Awake and arouse your faculties, even to an experiment upon my words."

Alma 32:27

Alma's Experiment with the Word

Alma begins by telling us that we need to "Exercise a particle of faith, yea, even if ye can no more than desire to believe, let this desire work in you, even until ye believe in a manner that ye can give place for a portion of my words" (Alma 32:27).

Let this desire to believe *work in you* until you are ready to try the experiment.

My niece told me that sometimes she doesn't want to read the scriptures or go to church. Her mom taught her when those times come, she needs to *pray for the want*. I love this. *Pray for the want.*

Because wanting to know what is true is the first step to gaining faith in the Book of Mormon. Having the desire to communicate with heaven is the first step to receiving revelation. This might take a while.

You may have to wrestle a little bit with this *desire to believe*. It's ok. Christ isn't going anywhere.

When you're ready—when the want is there,

"...we will compare the word unto a seed" (Alma 32:28).

This has tripped a few of us up over the years because of the primary song, "Faith." I don't think whoever wrote that song was trying to mess with our minds or throw us off course. The song never says they are singing about Alma's experiment. But the song says, "Faith is like a little seed; if planted it will grow."[44] Thus, in my mind, every time I read Alma 32 until just recently, I thought the experiment was planting the seed of faith.

But it's not, not at all. This is why I can say this experiment follows the scientific method because the results are measurable and discernable. We aren't experimenting with a vague word like faith; we are planting something tangible—the word. We are experimenting with the *words of Christ* found in the Book of Mormon.

I like to think of "giving place" for a portion of His words as digging a hole. The place we are going to dig the hole in is our hearts. We are going to plant the word of God deep in our hearts. Here is where this experiment begins.

We ask the question.

The questions we want to be answered might be, "Is this the word of God? Is the Book of Mormon really divine?" Lizzy's question is important to reiterate here. "I often wonder if my experience and life in the gospel and in general would be different had I been prideful or disingenuous."

With humility we ask, "Is this the word of God? Is the Book of Mormon really divine?" They are the questions of the century because if it is, then everything else that comes along with it is also true. It's such a fantastic question to ask. Because *if* the Book of Mormon is really the word of God, and it was translated directly by the power and authority of God through a living prophet, *then* I can stop obsessing over so many other questions.

For example, what people say Joseph Smith did or didn't do after the translation of the plates really doesn't matter to me. Because *if* the Book of Mormon is the word of God, *then* Joseph DID see Heavenly Father and Jesus Christ in the grove, and they *did* use him to bring this record to light. He was the first prophet of the restoration. The Gospel of Jesus Christ has been restored to the earth.

Do you think that because Joseph was called to be the first prophet of this dispensation, he was perfect? Please! Elder Holland clarified:

> Except in the case of His only perfect Begotten Son, imperfect people are all God has ever had to work with. That must be terribly frustrating to Him, but He deals with it. So should we. And when you see imperfection, remember that the limitation is not in the divinity of the work.[45]

I don't have to worry about Joseph Smith's perfection if the Book of Mormon is true. If I gain a testimony of the divinity of that book through this experiment, my testimony is not based on Joseph Smith. It's based on Jesus. It's based on the Holy Ghost. It's based on Heavenly Father and the love I feel from His words. The result of this experiment is life-changing. It can lay so many other questions to rest.

The question posed by Alma is this: "Is this the word of God?"

The next part of the scientific method is to form the hypothesis. We don't even have to do that because Alma already did.

It's our first if/then from Alma.

> ... behold, if it be a true seed, or a good seed, if ye do not cast it out by your unbelief, that ye will resist the Spirit of the Lord, behold, it will begin to swell within your breasts; and when you feel these swelling motions, ye will begin to say within yourselves—It must needs be that this is a good seed, or that the word is good, for it beginneth to enlarge my soul; yea, it beginneth to enlighten my understanding, yea, it beginneth to be delicious to me (Alma 32:28).

Make a space in our hearts for the word. If the word is good and true, it will enlarge our souls. It will feel good. It will begin to be delicious.

I have always felt a deep love for how Parley P. Pratt described his first encounter with reading the

Book of Mormon. He talked about reading all day. He said he didn't even want to eat or drink or sleep. He kept reading continually until he finished and knew without a doubt the book was true. He talked about the joy that filled his soul. He went on to be a powerful ambassador for the truth of the Gospel of Jesus Christ. He was a powerful missionary.[46]

Talk about delicious!

If the word is good and it starts teaching you things, and this pattern starts working, what happens? You don't immediately grow a tree, as you would expect from planting a seed. What does he say here? "It begins to enlighten your understanding" (Alma 32:28). It begins to be delicious.

This is what we want. We want to know that God is real and that all the sacrifices we make to serve Him are worth it. We want to hear His voice, and when we do, we want to hear it more and more. We begin to hunger and thirst after His word.

Alma then explained that after you've planted His words and it's good, things begin to feel good and right, *you know* that the seed is good. Because good seeds bring forth good fruit. It's a simple equation.

Alma next asked if the seed begins to grow and feels good and tastes good, doesn't this increase your faith? Yes. It does.

But, "Is your knowledge perfect?"

Alma answered.

> Yea, your knowledge is perfect in that thing, and your faith is dormant; and this because you know, for ye know that the word hath swelled your souls, and ye also know that it hath sprout-

ed up, that your understanding doth begin to be enlightened, and your mind doth begin to expand (Alma 32:43).

This is when we stop saying we hope the Book of Mormon is true, and we can begin to say we know it is because we've tried the test repeatedly. We've read it and let it sink deep into our hearts. We've come to it repentant and humble and have searched for answers and truth and for the warm guidance and reassurance of the Holy Ghost. We begin to receive answers and feel the light of Christ in our lives.

"O then, is not this real?"

"Yea, because it is light; and whatsoever is light, is good, because it is *discernible*, therefore ye must know that it is good;" (Alma 32:35 emphasis added).

This is your data. This enlightening—this warmth and joy, these answers to your questions, this is your data. This discernible light that comes into your heart—it's part of the data. Your hypothesis is confirmed again and again. But only if you return to it again and again. Because Alma tells the people, when you start feeling the goodness of the word of God, you can't stop.

"Let us nourish it with great care, that it may get root, that it may grow up, and bring forth fruit unto us. And now behold, if ye nourish it with much care it will get root, and grow up, and bring forth fruit" (Alma 32:37).

How do we nourish the word with great care? I think the first thing is to return often. Like, every single day.

I have had a few real plants in my life. I'm sad to say that I forget to water them. One day I'll look and see one is almost dead. I'll quickly pull off the dead leaves, give it some water, and watch and wait. Sometimes it will revive. But most of the time, I've neglected it for too long, and it dies. Even though I love how natural plants look, I need to be reminded to water them. I just get distracted. No matter how much I love a live plant, it will die if I don't take care of it. It's a fact.

So it is with faith and our attention to the word of God.

> But if ye neglect the tree, and take no thought for its nourishment, behold it will not get any root; and when the heat of the sun cometh and scorcheth it, because it hath no root it withers away, and ye pluck it up and cast it out. Now, this is not because the seed was not good, neither is it because the fruit thereof would not be desirable; but it is because your ground is barren, and ye will not nourish the tree, therefore ye cannot have the fruit thereof (Alma 32:38).

There's a parable in the fourth chapter of Mark called the Parable of the Sower. Jesus explained what happens when we don't put down strong enough roots:

> And these are they likewise which are sown on stony ground; who, when they have heard the word, immediately receive it with gladness; And

have no root in themselves, and so endure but for a time: afterward, when affliction or persecution ariseth for the word's sake, immediately they are offended (Mark 4:16-17).

I think this is such an easy place to be. We hear the gospel taught by the missionaries or we grew up in the church and have a good relationship or feeling about the gospel. It has brought us joy. It has made us happy. Perhaps we've even had a spiritual experience or two that have helped us to believe that Heavenly Father is real or the church is true. But daily, we aren't doing anything more to secure that testimony. We casually go to church each week, thinking we are diligent and firmly planted in our faith. But when the storms come or persecutions arise, it says we are "immediately offended."

We don't want this. You don't want this. To avoid this, you need to be "rooting" yourself to the Savior. This happens when we feast daily on the words of Christ. This happens when we minister to others and when we listen to conference talks again and again. It happens as we magnify our callings and daily do the small and simple things that don't seem like a big deal. But they are a big deal. You don't realize that you send roots down deeper into the earth every time you read or pray so that you won't topple or be "immediately offended" when the storms come. Another byproduct of this is that you also know where to turn to find peace when the storms do come.

I like imagery. Maybe because I'm quickly losing my mind and forget everything almost immediately after hearing or reading it. But if I see a picture of something in my mind, it helps me remember it.

I remember experimenting with seeds in grade school. Or maybe I just remember my kids' experiments because, inevitably, they spilled in the car or on my carpet, and I had to clean them up. The first one was a white Styrofoam® cup with some soil in it that you shoved a seed into and then waited for it to sprout. Whatever seeds we used, I think it was a bean of some sort, always sprouted pretty quickly. Kids have no patience for seeds that take more than two days to sprout. We would water this little cup of dirt and put it in the sun, and a few days later, we would see a little sprout push its way out of the soil. This was exciting to us and made us want to keep watering it. It eventually got big enough that we understood the process: plant a seed and take care of it, and it will grow.

The other experiment put the same kind of seed in a plastic Ziploc® bag with some water and a paper towel. Moms prefer this method because it keeps our minivans much cleaner. The same thing would happen, but in the bag method, you can see what is happening on the other side of the seed, the part under the dirt. You can also see the roots that are growing down from the seed. And we see the roots *before* the sprout.

Now, this is where the imagery will depart from what you remember. Instead of the roots jutting down into the dirt, I want you to imagine a long metal pole below the surface. Each time you read the scriptures, you send down roots that slowly wrap around that pole. Every time you read, especially when you do it as I taught with praying and repenting and pondering, you send roots down that wrap around and around that pole, every time. Maybe you don't see any sprouts on the surface. You may not think anything is even happening. But every time, you are securing your roots to that rod.

Now one more stretch of the imagination is necessary. I want you to imagine that rod is Jesus Christ. Each time you purposefully turn to the words of Christ in the scriptures, you are securing your testimony, your seed, your faith, to Jesus Christ. This is why it's so important to do it every day! One wrap of a root around anything isn't going to hold when the winds blow. But a testimony secured to the Savior by thousands of roots grown over years of attentive care will hold firm no matter what storms are hurled at it.

When a giant storm comes, does a tree quickly untangle its roots and hang on to a light post or a bench? Of course not! So, it is with us. If we have rooted ourselves to the Savior by daily planting the word in our hearts, when the storm comes, we cling to what we are rooted to—the Savior. That's why I was able to make the statement at the beginning with so much assurance. Daily immersing ourselves in the word of God creates a root system that will not fail us. It just won't.

I love this image. When you get done reading every night, you can say, "That's a wrap." Maybe you can imagine the iron rod in Lehi's dream. You can't wander off into forbidden paths or even get to the spacious building. You would have to untie way too much to leave. It's so good. I love it.

Nephi promised us that those who hold tight to the iron rod "would never perish; neither could the temptations and the fiery darts of the adversary overpower them unto blindness, to lead them away to destruction" (1 Nephi 15:24). It isn't hard to hold tight when you've bound yourself to the iron rod. You become less and less tempted to head off course.

One time I spoke at our stake's Relief Society conference. I told many of my experiences where the Lord answered my prayers so directly through scriptures. I have had some really powerful experiences. The Spirit was there. It was a good night.

The next day was fast Sunday, and a woman got up to bear her testimony. She began by saying that when she heard me speak, she felt sad that she had not had any miraculous experiences like I had, where she heard the voice of the Lord so clearly. Then she shared this beautiful insight. "I got to thinking about the last two years. They have probably been the hardest years of my life. Our financial situation changed, and I had to go back to work." She rehearsed some other trials that had beset her over this period. And then she said, "What if I hadn't been reading every night over these past two years? What if I had neglected this one thing? Those trials would have overwhelmed me, and I may have lost my faith."

That whole time she was wrapping herself around Christ and the protection of His word. She was developing a root system that she couldn't see but was real.

Now that we understand what is going on beneath the surface when we read, let's get back to Alma.

And behold, as the tree beginneth to grow, ye will say: Let us nourish it with great care, that it may get root, that it may grow up, and bring forth fruit unto us. And now behold, if ye nourish it with much care it will get root, and grow up, and bring forth fruit. And because of your diligence and your faith and your patience with the word in nourishing it, that it may take root in you, behold, by and by ye shall pluck the fruit thereof, which is most precious, which is sweet above all that is sweet, and which is white above all that is white, yea, and pure above all that is pure; and ye shall feast upon this fruit even until ye are filled, that ye hunger not, neither shall ye thirst (Alma 32:37, 42).

What's this fruit? What is the reward we are waiting for as we nourish our faith with the word of God?

Lehi describes it as a "fruit that was desirable to make one happy." After he tasted it, he proclaimed, "it filled my soul with exceedingly great joy."

Nephi clarified, "it is the love of God, which sheddeth itself abroad in the hearts of the children of men; wherefore, it is the most desirable above all things ... Yea, and the most joyous to the soul" (1 Nephi 11:22).

This is the reason I wrote this book. This is the reason I return again and again to the Book of Mormon. It's all about joy. Feeling the love of God on a continual basis feels better than anything else.

Hang on. Keep reading, even if you don't see any sprouts right now.

"Then, my brethren, ye shall reap the rewards of your faith, and your diligence, and patience, and long-suffering, waiting for the tree to bring forth fruit unto you" (Alma 32:43).

"Behold it shall be a tree springing up unto everlasting life" (Alma 32:41).

CHAPTER 22

"Long before the world was formed, Satan and those who followed after him raged against the forces of good and tried to overthrow the work of God. That struggle has not ended, only shifted battlegrounds. It is ruthless and relentless, and the objective of the battle is your eternal soul and mine."

Elder M. Russell Ballard

I'm going to be super blunt here as I finish this up because I'm not one to throw happy, little platitudes at you, pat your head, and send you on your way. I care too much about all of you to do that. This is serious stuff, and I want to end with some serious caution.

At this point, we have two choices: we can continue to nourish the sprout and take good care of it, or we can neglect it to the point where it can't take root, and it dies.

If we've tasted the love of God that can be found in His word, and it is good—delicious even—why would we ever neglect it?

I told you that I love donuts. It's a big problem. I want to eat a donut any time of day, any chance I get. It will take great willpower to not have one by the end of the day because I mentioned it here. My mind will chant, "Donut! Donut! Donut!" until I leave my house and go get one.

So why, if I have the ability to partake of something that I know is delicious, why would I stop? Especially if it's practically in my hands at all times during the day?

Because Satan is a jerk, and he knows that this little experiment will save your spiritual life. He'll do all he can to keep you from continually reading. We have to be on guard and tell him to back off every single day. Unfortunately, he's never going to back down. He knows that the Book of Mormon is the one thing that will continually convert us day in and day out for the rest of our lives. He knows this reading plan ties us to our Savior. He knows that we can see through his ploys every time when we dive in and make studying a daily habit. We can't give up. We have to return every day.

One time when our kids were young, we had a family home evening about stranger danger. A girl had recently been kidnapped, and there was some video footage of the kidnapping. She basically just walked behind a convenience store with a stranger, and he grabbed her and threw her in his car and was gone. She didn't survive.

We wanted to show our kids that you had to fight back. If someone is trying to steal you, you kick and scream and yell, "This person is not my dad!" Bite, fight, do whatever you must do not to be taken.

Then my husband proceeded to try to kidnap our kids in the family room. The kids fought and kicked and did all they could to get away.

When FHE was over, my son, who was about ten at the time, looked at us, and said, "That was the freakiest family home evening ever. I'm scared out of my pants!"

Sorry, folks. Sometimes we have to be scared out of our pants in order to be aware of the danger. We need to know what we are facing in order to make a plan. Elder M. Russell Ballard warned:

> Long before the world was formed, Satan and those who followed after him raged against the forces of good and tried to overthrow the work of God. That struggle has not ended, only shifted battlegrounds. It is ruthless and relentless, and the objective of the battle is your eternal soul and mine.[47]

Satan wants us. He will try everything to stop us from forming a relationship with the Savior and learning to hear His voice.

In the first area of my mission, we taught a girl named Yuki. She was so great. When we met her, she was an atheist. It was such a treat to see someone go from not believing in anything to embracing all the beautiful truths of the gospel. Her appreciation for the Savior was contagious. Although my Japanese was so limited at that time, the few words we exchanged were so tender to me. When she came up out of the waters of baptism, I was there holding a towel for her. She looked at me with a smile and said, "Ureshii!" I knew that word! It meant happy. I nodded, and we laughed. "Ureshii!" I said. I felt it too.

When she decided to be baptized, we warned her that Satan would try everything to keep her from getting baptized. "Watch out!" we warned. The week before someone's baptism always ends up being a challenge. There were always things that would happen to try to impede the pending baptism day. On the day of Yuki's baptism, at the appointed time, she didn't show up. As we waited, we got more worried. "Oh no! Maybe she changed her mind." Minutes ticked past. Finally, she pulled into the church parking lot on her scooter. She carefully got off the bike and kind of hobbled over to us. She had a Band-Aid® on her face and a few fingers were taped together.

"What happened?" we asked in concern. She looked at us and said, "You said Satan was going to try to stop me. You didn't say he was going to try to *kill* me."

The day before, she had been hit on her scooter and had ended up at the hospital. Thankfully she was ok. And although she was joking about the murder business, she realized that it had definitely been a roadblock. She almost didn't make it to her baptism.

Don't ever forget that Satan wants us all miserable like he is. And he knows sooo well that if you study the scriptures like this every day, he loses so much power. He doesn't want you to make this a habit. Not at all.

Remember what happened when Joseph Smith went to the grove to pray? Right before our Heavenly Father and Jesus Christ appeared to him, he described kneeling down to pray. He recounted:

> After I had retired to the place where I had previously designed to go, having looked around me, and finding myself alone, I kneeled down and began to offer up the desires of my heart to God. I had scarcely done so, when immediately I was seized upon by some power which entirely overcame me, and had such an astonishing influence over me as to bind my tongue so that I could not speak. Thick darkness gathered around me, and it seemed to me for a time as if I were doomed to sudden destruction. But, exerting all my powers to call upon God to deliver me out of the power of this enemy which had seized upon me, and at the very moment when I was ready to sink into despair and abandon myself to destruction—not to an imaginary ruin, but to the power of some actual being from the unseen world, who had such marvelous power as I had never before felt in any being—just at this moment of great alarm, I saw a pillar of light exactly over my head, above the brightness of the sun...[48]

We know the rest of the story. [Maybe you don't. Maybe you are not a member of The Church of Jesus Christ of Latter-day Saints. If you've read this far, you might want to contact some missionaries and have them come tell you the rest and bring you your very own free copy of the Book of Mormon. (https://www.churchofjesuschrist.org/comeuntochrist)]

My mom says this part of The First Vision helps her know it's true. Why would a fourteen-year-old make up the part about the darkness right before the light? She has such a good point. It seems like a detail a kid wouldn't add to a fantastic story about seeing God.

Right before our Heavenly Father and Jesus Christ came to bring all that light and love back into the world, Satan tried to stop it. Satan didn't get off Joseph's back his whole life. Satan knew all the good that was going to come from Joseph Smith and the souls he would save. Satan never relented.

What important things were you sent to this earth to do? Do you think Satan wants you to become all you can? Do you think he wants you to study the Book of Mormon every day? He definitely doesn't want you to learn to hear the Savior's voice. He wants to keep you confused.

In the New Testament, it says, "My sheep hear my voice, and I know them, and they follow me" (John 10:27). I have learned to hear the Master's voice by turning to the Book of Mormon daily. I recognize it, and I turn to Him to keep me safe. It's harder for Satan to trick me because his voice isn't the one I've come to trust. In John chapter 10, we learn what happens when people try to trick Christ's sheep.

Christ explained:

> Verily verily I say unto you, He that entereth not by the door into the sheep fold, but climbeth up some other way, the same is a thief and a robber. But he that entereth in by the door is the shepherd of the sheep... and the

sheep hear His voice and he calls his own sheep by name and leadeth them out. And when he put it forth his own sheep he goeth before them, and the sheep follow them, for they know His voice and a stranger will they not follow, but will flee from him, for they know not the voice of strangers (John 10:1-5).

We are His sheep. We can learn to hear His voice.

"You can't trick me, Satan. That's not my Shepherd's voice. You are a stranger. And I won't follow you because I don't follow the voice of strangers."

This reminds me of that story that my cool Grandma Tot used to tell us up at that cabin of ours when I was small—you know, the one I freaked out my neighbor kids with? It's about a mother goat and her seven kids. Ya, baby goats are called kids. Did you know that? Did you know that a young platypus is called a puggle? And a baby salamander is called a salamanderling?

You're welcome.

This mother goat has to go to town to get some groceries, and there is a wolf that is trying to get in and eat her babies. He's always trying to trick them. So she gives her kids some instructions before she leaves. She says, "If someone knocks on the door, ask who it is. Listen carefully to the voice. If it's a rough voice, then you know it's the wolf. But if it's a soft voice, then you know it's me." The wolf comes, and he doesn't trick them at first, but he never stops trying to get them. Eventually, they get all confused. They don't pay close enough attention, and he gets in and eats them all, except for the kid who hid in the grandfather clock.

Now, there isn't time to tell the whole story, but don't worry. The wolf quickly ate those baby goats whole, so hours later, when the sole remaining goat shows Mom where the wolf is napping, the mother quietly cuts that wolf's belly open with scissors, and all the babies jump right out, safe and sound! Hahahahahaha. What a story!

But unlike those little goat babies who got tricked, over time, we can really discern what the Savior's voice sounds and *feels* like. We can pay attention. When the adversary comes trying to deceive us, we can say, "Wait, wait, wait! I know the Savior's voice because I listen to Him all the time. I read the scriptures, and I try to do what He says. This voice that's talking right now—that's not my Savior's voice. That's not my Shepherd's voice. I'm not gonna listen to you. You're a stranger here."

The more we listen to Jesus, and the more we look to Him as our Shepherd, we're not going to be deceived.

CHAPTER 23

"Put on the whole armour of God, that ye may be able to stand against the wiles of the devil. For we wrestle not against flesh and blood, but against principalities, against powers, against the rulers of the darkness of this world, against spiritual wickedness in high places."

Ephesians 6:11-12

L ike that family home evening, that scripture should scare you a little. That's a lot of forces working against us. But it's ok. We have some help at our disposal—the armor of God.

> Wherefore take unto you the whole armour of God, that ye may be able to withstand in the evil day. ... Stand therefore, having your loins girt about with truth, and having on the breastplate of righteousness; And your feet shod with the preparation of the gospel of peace; Above all, taking the shield of faith, wherewith ye shall be able to quench all the fiery darts of the wicked. And take the helmet of salvation, and the

sword of the Spirit, which is the word of God; Praying always with all prayer and supplication in the Spirit (Ephesians 6:13–18).

If we learn to use this armor, we will be better protected in this ongoing war against the adversary and all his scary helpers.

What is the piece of armor that covers our most vital organs, our heart and lungs? Righteousness. Keeping the commandments is one of the very best protections we can put up against the devil. It is the reason that we read one million times in the Book of Mormon that if we keep the commandments, we'll prosper in the land. When we strictly keep the commandments, without being Pharisaical about it, we are doing the number one thing we can do to protect ourselves against the wiles of the devil. Think about the song "Keep the Commandments." It ends with the line, "Keep the commandments; in this there is safety and peace."[49] It's so true.

Another cool thing about obedience is that it's contagious. In the last area of my mission, I served with a Japanese companion. I'll call her Sister Tanaka. She was a new missionary, and she was awesome. One night we had multiple appointments, which all involved food of some kind. By the third appointment, we were so stuffed. We decided to have an "eat till you barf" competition. We shoved and shoved so much food down, laughing all the while. I remember getting back to our apartment, and as I lifted one more piece of food to my mouth, she started to gag. I think I won. Wasn't I a great trainer?

I mentioned earlier that we rode bikes our whole mission; sisters on bikes, in dresses, with helmets. It was glorious. And by glorious, I mean the worst. I got my skirts caught in my chain more times than I can count. Once, we were speeding along with our whole district somewhere, and my skirt got caught in my chain so violently that my skirt tore completely off my waist. Luckily, I had on a long winter coat that covered me as the elders untangled and freed the fabric.

As bad as skirts in chains were, wearing a helmet was worse. It was humid all the time, and donning a helmet did wonders for our hairdos. Plus, no one in the entire country wore helmets except the missionaries. And while that was good advertising I guess, it was embarrassing, and I hate to admit that sometimes I didn't wear it, especially in the hot, humid summer.

One morning Sister Tanaka and I studied obedience in our companionship study, and then we left to go begin proselyting. It apparently had rained overnight, and our helmets, which we casually hung on the handlebars of our bike, had filled with water. I dumped mine out, hung it back over the handlebar, and started riding down the lane that led from our apartment to the street. As I looked back, my companion wasn't following me. After a bit, I turned back to see what was keeping her.

Sister Tanaka was standing next to her bike, with her handkerchief, gently blotting the water out of it. As she picked it up and put it on her head, water dripped down her face and onto her shoulders. I asked her what she was doing. Her reply was a lesson that sunk deep into my soul.

"Sister, this morning we learned about obedience."

I lifted my helmet off my handlebars, dumped out the water, and I too put my helmet on. Water dripped off my face as I drove off. Maybe that was a good thing, for it hid my tears.

"For as by one man's disobedience many were made sinners, so by the obedience of one shall many be made righteous" (Rom. 5:19).

I learned an important lesson from my sweet, Japanese companion. If we really love the Lord, we don't pick and choose what commandments we feel like keeping each day. We should do our best to keep them all.

I don't remember what my hair looked or smelled like that day, but I'll always remember the love and admiration I had for Sister Tanaka and her courage to be obedient.

I was going to write one last chapter all about obedience, but since we are here discussing it now, I'll round out my thoughts about it.

If you want the Lord to speak to you through the pages of scripture, you have to do your best to be worthy to have the Holy Ghost with you. The Holy Ghost is the person who whispers the messages from Heavenly Father and Jesus Christ to you. If you don't have the Holy Ghost with you, it is very, very hard to hear Their messages.

Sure, in an emergency or in a time of deep despair, the Lord can answer your prayers this way and help you feel His love. But if you want this method to work daily, you must step up your obedience game.

Elder M. Russell Ballard said:

> The stunning reality, my dear young brothers and sisters, is that you control how close you are to the Lord. You determine just how clear and readily available promptings from the Holy Ghost will be. You determine this by your actions, by your attitude, by the choices you make, by the things you watch and wear and listen to and read, and by how consistently and sincerely you invite the Spirit into your life.[50]

When I started the podcast, I realized very quickly that Satan wasn't jazzed about it. It was a nightmare every week to keep him off my back. The quicker the podcast spread, the more relentless he was about trying to pull me away from the Spirit.

I realized I had to be stricter about what I watched on TV, and I had to return the Audible books when they became full of swears. I had to try harder to get along with people and apologize when I was wrong. I had to be more diligent. I got a little insight into how a stake patriarch must feel. I had to keep my life clean and follow the rules because I didn't want to say a bunch of false doctrine, and I truly wanted to be open to the whisperings of the Spirit. If there was something that needed to be said to touch that one person, then I needed to know.

The more vigilant I became about being more strictly obedient, the more I noticed that Satan had less and less power to knock me off course. I began to see more and more miracles in my life. My capacity to hear the whisperings of the Spirit and receive revelation increased. There was more peace in my life and calm in my soul.

Elder Corbridge said in one of my favorite talks of all time, *Stand Forever*:

> Pay whatever price you must pay, bear whatever burden you must bear, and make whatever sacrifice you must make to get and keep in your life the spirit and power of the Holy Ghost. Every good thing depends on getting and keeping the power of the Holy Ghost in your life. Everything depends on that.[51]

It's too scary out there. Too many people are getting distracted and confused and wandering off. I don't want that! Neither do you.

I've noticed another thing happens as I try harder to keep the commandments more exactly in my life—I prosper in the land. We read it a zillion times in the Book of Mormon. The Lord promises over and over that when you keep the commandments, He blesses you.

Joseph Smith taught us in the Doctrine and Covenants, "There is a law, irrevocably decreed in heaven before the foundations of this world, upon which all blessings are predicated—and when we obtain any blessing from God, it is by obedience to that law upon which it is predicated" (Doctrine and Covenants 130:20–21).

This doesn't always mean you get the house, or your marriage stays together. It doesn't mean that your dad doesn't die, or your sisters don't get cancer. It doesn't mean that all your kids will keep the faith or that you won't slip and twist your ankle, choke on a chicken bone, or accidentally pee your pants from laughing so hard at camp.

But what it does mean is that you can still feel peace and joy even when all of that is happening. It means that you can lean on the Lord whenever you need to because He'll be so close to you. President Nelson said:

> My dear brothers and sisters, the joy we feel has little to do with the circumstances of our lives and everything to do with the focus of our lives. When the focus of our lives is on God's plan of salvation, and Jesus Christ and His gospel, we can feel joy regardless of what is happening—or not happening—in our lives. Joy comes from and because of Him. He is the source of all joy.[52]

I think this life is like one of those choose-your-own-adventure books we had when we were kids. So much of where our journey leads us depends on our righteousness. We may not even know what blessings the Lord gave us when we took out our second set of earrings or walked out of that dirty movie. But maybe He poured down an extra blessing on you that day. Maybe you didn't slip on that ice, or you did better on your test.

We won't always know what righteous choices led us to what outcomes. When we sin, a lot of times the consequences of those choices are more apparent: I wrote my own prescription, and now I'm in jail.

I hope in some of our after-this-life activities, we get to see some of the blessings that we got from obedience that we never realized.

Maybe you'll hear something like this. "Remember that day when you went to church and kept the Sabbath Day holy instead of going to Krispy Kreme like you really wanted to? The next day your son came home and apologized for that fight you were in. That was because *you* were obedient."

"Remember that day when you chose to be kind to your brother instead of punching his face like you wanted to? That very next week, your dad changed his mind and bought that puppy you'd been begging for. *That* was because you chose the right."

I'm not sure that will happen. I don't know what goes on after this life. But I hope we can see a little more of those things. They would be so fun to discover, much more fun than seeing all the times I saw what I needed to do and straightway forgot.

Sometimes we get to see the blessings in this life. My daughter and her husband were struggling with some money problems. They had to pay their tithing, and they were reluctant. They really needed the money. They decided to pay it, and shortly thereafter, they got a check in the mail for way more than the cost of the tithing. All because some company hadn't hired him because they were looking for a native Spanish speaker. Someone got mad, cried foul, and the company got sued for discrimination. Her husband got a check in the mail for the difference between what he got paid at the menial job he had at that time, and what he would have been paid at that doctor's office.

Tithing is such a cool obedience principle because, so often, we see the blessing right away. I could write chapters on the blessings I've seen from paying my tithing. But my point is that we are not going to hell for not going to church when we are on vacation. I'm sure the devil won't be waiting at the elevator to take us straight down to the fire for finding one more excuse not to wear our garments to the next activity. But what blessings are we missing that the Lord is waiting to pour down on those who show their love for Him by doing what He says? We may never know.

My friend Emily said to me the other day, "Jesus's love language has always been obedience." She's right, you know. You don't have to look very far to find this truth. "If ye love me, keep my commandments" (John 14:15).

Once when my two oldest kids were very little, they were fighting and driving me nuts. I kept asking them to stop, and they wouldn't. Noticing my frustration, my daughter, who was almost four at the time, said to me, "I love you, Mommy." In exasperation, I said, "If you loved me, you would do what I say."

At that moment, God gave me a little glimpse of how He feels. "If ye love me, keep my commandments." Jesus continues by saying, "He that hath my commandments, and keepeth them, he it is that loveth me: and he that loveth me shall be loved of my Father, and I will love him, and will manifest myself to him" (John 14:21).

Manifest means, "To show plainly; to make to appear distinctly, –usually to the mind; to put beyond question or doubt."[53] I want Christ to show Himself so plainly to me that I won't doubt or question His reality. He doesn't say, "I don't love you if you don't keep My commandments." He loves us all. But He does say He'll manifest Himself to those who are obedient. That's what we are looking for.

The more obedient we are, the more blessings we get. I could go on forever!

> And truth is knowledge of things as they are, and as they were, and as they are to come; ... And no man receiveth a fulness unless he keepeth his commandments. He that keepeth his commandments receiveth truth and light, until he is glorified in truth and knoweth all things. (Doctrine and Covenants 93:24, 26-28)

What are the things we want to know most? What color pillow would look fabulous on our new couch? Which place has the best sushi in town? Or, how do I get back home to live with my Heavenly Father and Jesus Christ forever? How do I overcome this sadness? How do handle this trial?

President Gordon B. Hinckley said:

> The happiness of the Latter-day Saints, the peace of the Latter-day Saints, the progress of the Latter-day Saints, the prosperity of the Latter-day Saints, and the eternal salvation and exaltation of this people lie in walking in obedience to the counsels of ... God.[54]

This process of trying hard to keep the commandments, repenting when I don't, praying, and turning to the scriptures again and again helped me find the Savior. Every time a specific scripture answers a prayer, gives me comfort, or brings me peace, I'm more and more grateful for His grace and the love I feel. I *want* to keep the commandments. I want to return all that love in *His* love language, which has always been obedience.

One night I got to a stoplight that was out in a busy intersection in my hometown. It wasn't flashing; it was just out. It was pandemonium. Some people were edging out, trying to see if it was their turn to go. Others were just zooming through, arrogantly thinking it was their right of way, even if no one knew whose right of way it even was. I felt really unsafe and hated that intersection and experience. I just wanted the light back on or for a policeman to get in the street and tell us what to do. I like the tidy boundary of rules that keep me safe.

My sister said once that trying to live without commandments is like playing tennis on your driveway instead of on a court. You spend most of the game running down the street after the balls and so much less time actually enjoying the game. The boundaries of that fence around the court actually make playing the game easier.

Contrary to what you might think, commandments aren't given by some big kill-joy in heaven that doesn't want us to have any fun. They are given to us so that we can find joy and avoid so many pitfalls.

Elder Von G. Keetch said,

> The Lord's commands do not constitute some grueling underwater maze of barriers that we must learn to grudgingly endure in this life so that we might be exalted in the next. Rather, the barriers established by the Lord create for us a safe harbor from the evil and destructive influences that would otherwise drag us down to the depths of despair. The Lord's commandments are given out of love and caring; they are intended for our joy in this life just as much as they are intended for our joy and exaltation in the next. They mark the way that we should act—and more importantly, they illuminate who we should become.[55]

Some commandments make a lot of sense to me. Don't kill. If I do, it's going to be bad for me and is guaranteed to ruin at least one other person's day. Don't commit adultery. It can break hearts and mess up families. Don't steal, bear false witness, or smoke the drugs. I get those things.

But the counsel to dress in modest clothing, or watch my language? Why shouldn't I go buy the donuts on Sunday? Do I always have to be fully honest— even if the situation will ensure I receive some much needed money?

There are a lot of these kinds of rules and guidelines that I might not understand. But Elder Maxwell said something once that burrowed its way deep into my heart when I heard it. I'll never forget it.

"... we will not always understand the role of God's hand, but we know enough of his heart and mind to be submissive."[56] This is where I've come to be in my life. All the times I've turned to the Savior, He's had my back. He blessed my circumstances where He could or cheered my heart when He couldn't change my situation. He's the best friend I have in the world. I know, to my very center, that He only wants what's best for me. So like Elder Maxwell said, I don't have to understand every rule and all He asks of me. I know what kind of person He is. If He asks me to do something, it's because He loves me. I can do what He asks because I know my happiness is always His end game. Always.

An elder said something when I was a missionary in Japan that I think about a lot. I'm not sure if he thought it up or was quoting someone else, but I wrote it down. He said we should be obedient "not in search of blessings, nor in fear of punishment, but in deep gratitude, to glorify Him."

We may start doing what the Lord has asked of us because we don't want to go to hell. We might be scared. Or we might be searching for all the things God will do for us if we are good. These things are good motivators. I'm not saying they aren't. But when you follow His guidance long enough, when you develop a relationship with the Creator of the universe, you may just get to a point where you do what He asks simply because you love Jesus so much.

The Prophet's wife, Wendy Nelson, said something so important in an interview with Sherri Dew for the *Church News* podcast:

> I think it's not an accident that we are im-
> mersed in the waters of baptism ... If after be-
> ing immersed, we then only sprinkle our lives
> with a little scripture here, a little prayer there,
> a little fasting there, we will only know enough
> about the gospel to feel guilty and not enough
> to feel joy.[57]

This is HUGE. So many of us are stuck with guilt and only feeling what we perceive as all the *restrictions* that the gospel supposedly puts on us. If you're there, spend more time in the scriptures. Be more strictly obedient, even when you think you don't want anyone telling you what to do. You will come to know your Father in Heaven and Jesus Christ more intimately. As you close the gap between you and Them, your motives and desires will shift, and you will *want* to be better. Your heart will change. The Holy Ghost will be your constant companion, and you will feel so much more joy in your life.

There's my two cents on obedience. Felt more like $29.99. Sheesh!

We were talking about the armor of God, remember? I didn't, either. But here we are. Haha.

Paul suggests a few more pieces of armor that will keep us safe in this relentless battle. He suggests covering our feet with the preparation of the gospel of peace. What does this mean? What do we use our feet for in battle? How do we prepare? We study the gospel. This includes things such as seminary, going to church, and reading the scriptures at home by yourself and with your family. It includes studying

Come Follow Me and watching and re-listening and reading General Conference twice a year. The more you know, the quicker you'll be able to recognize falsehoods and Satan's traps. Knowledge is literally power when it comes to fighting the adversary.

I also think it's very telling that Paul wrote the gospel of PEACE.

We live in a world today where arguing about anything and everything has become the norm. I had to walk away from Facebook during the last few months of the last election because I couldn't believe the things that people were saying to each other. Phrases like, "agree to disagree" were replaced by, "If you believe in any candidate besides my favorite candidate, then you are the literal spawn of Satan, and it is now my new goal to annihilate you." It was a bloodbath over there.

When Paul describes covering our feet with peace, I also think it means walking out of the room when peace turns to contention. Study and learn the peaceable things of the kingdom, and don't settle for less.

I wasted a lot of time in my life fighting against those who were fighting against the church. Do you know who wins in that battle 98% of the time? Satan. Satan is the father of contention, and even if we are defending our faith, if we get in that arena and it gets contentious, we lose. I thought I was choosing the right by arguing points of doctrine about the prophet Joseph Smith and the Book of Mormon as often as I did. But when it turned into a brawl, I lost. You can't scream, "Joseph was a prophet of the Lord, you big jerk!" and think that you're standing on the Lord's side.

Elder Holland gave some great advice on the subject. "Be strong. Live the gospel faithfully even if others around you don't live it at all. Defend your beliefs with courtesy and with compassion, but defend them."[58]

Courtesy and compassion—do you know what this looks like? "I'm so sorry you feel that way about Joseph Smith. I love him. I'm so grateful for him. Without him, I wouldn't have the Book of Mormon, and the Book of Mormon saved my spiritual life." Bearing pure testimony is the best way to defend our faith. And if it starts to turn into a battle, put on those spiritual Nikes that Paul talked about and head out of the room.

Sometimes we think being meek is a sign of weakness. But Elder Ulisses Soares explains otherwise. He said:

Meekness is vital for us to become more Christlike. Without it we won't be able to develop other important virtues. Being meek does not mean weakness, but it does mean behaving with goodness and kindness, showing strength, serenity, healthy self-worth, and self-control.[59]

When Jesus Christ was sitting on a hillside preaching to the people, He gave them some great advice about being a peacemaker. He said:

Blessed are the peacemakers: for they shall be called the children of God. Blessed are they which are persecuted for righteousness' sake: for theirs is the kingdom of heaven. Blessed are ye, when men shall revile you, and persecute you, and shall say all manner of evil against you falsely, for my sake. Rejoice, and be exceeding glad: for great is your reward in heaven: for so persecuted they the prophets which were before you (Matthew 5:9-12).

It's hard to rejoice and be exceedingly glad when someone is treating you unfairly because of your beliefs. You hardly feel like exclaiming, "Yea! Keep telling me how dumb I am. This is soo great. I love it. Best day ever!"

But I'm pretty sure that isn't what Jesus was suggesting.

President Wilford Woodruff added clarity to this idea when he said, "I do not think we should complain because if we had no trials we should hardly feel at home in the other world in the company of the Prophets and Apostles who were sawn asunder, crucified, etc., for the word of God and testimony of Jesus Christ."[60]

When Christ told the people to rejoice and be exceedingly glad, I think He was saying, "Be glad. You're in great company. Some of the very best humans ever were also persecuted for My sake. It's like an elite club. Not everyone will be able to sit at that table. But you will."

My son, Blake, is a peacemaker. He tries to put down contention wherever he finds it. When people are having a hard time, he tries to fix it. He extends the kind word, gives people the benefit of the doubt, and if that doesn't work, he puts you in his car and takes you to Dairy Queen. Everyone wants to be around him.

It broke all our hearts when he went away to college.

I think I changed my mind. Don't be a peacemaker. Be a jerk. It will make it a lot easier for your mom when you finally grow up and leave home.

Wow, that was a lot on those spiritual Nikes. That is a piece of armor that I have glossed over many times. The world is a contentious place right now, and contention is one of Satan's most cunning, traps—particularly when he can get us fighting about religion. That is what a wile of the devil is—a stratagem or trick intended to deceive or ensnare. Remember Wild E. Coyote? He was that cartoon character that was always trying to push Roadrunner off cliffs and drop anvils and such on him. So when you think of the wiles of the devil, imagine a giant anvil over your head. Outsmart him!

Beep Beep.

The next piece of spiritual armor that Paul talks about is the shield of faith. I like the image of a shield because you can constantly move it around you to protect yourself from the enemy.

When I think of faith, and lots of it, I think of David, the David who fights Goliath. He wasn't even a soldier; he was a shepherd, but his brothers were part of the Israelite army, and they were in trouble. A huge giant named Goliath had come to them and was ready to fight all who dared. Problem was, no one dared.

Up walked tiny David. I call him tiny because it makes for a better story. I'm not sure how big he was, but he wasn't a giant, and we've established he wasn't a soldier. Goliath laughed as he saw him approach. It was probably a laughable sight, the young David standing before a giant with nothing but a slingshot and a few pebbles. But David's strength wasn't coming from his weapon—it was coming from his faith. He looked up at Goliath and probably had to shout. "Thou comest to me with a sword, and with a spear, and with a shield; but I come to thee in the name of the Lord of hosts, the God of the armies of Israel, whom thou hast defied" (1 Sam. 17:45). Then David picked up the stone, swung it around, and killed the giant.

There was a VeggieTales cartoon that my kids watched way too many times when they were small. That counts, right? If I have the songs memorized, then they must too. It's in them, right? Haha.

It talked about how God was bigger than all the things that scare kids: monsters, boogie men, Godzilla, etc. Whenever I think of David, I hear that song. When trials or temptations or obstacles seem too big, that is when we have to have faith in a God that is bigger.

Neil L. Anderson said:

Faith does not fall upon us by chance or stay with us by birthright. It is, as the scriptures say, 'substance ..., the evidence of things not seen.' Faith emits a spiritual light, and that light is discernible. Faith in Jesus Christ is a gift from heaven that comes as we choose to believe and as we seek it and hold on to it. Your faith is either growing stronger or becoming weaker.

Faith is a principle of power, important not only in this life but also in our progression beyond the veil. By the grace of Christ, we will one day be saved through faith on His name. The future of your faith is not by chance, but by choice.[61]

Let that statement sink in for a minute. Sometimes people wait until there is a reason to have faith. "I will have faith when..." Elder Anderson is admonishing us to have faith now. Decide to have faith. Decide to believe right now. God will pour down so many more blessings to the faithful than He can to those waiting to see the blessings before they will believe. There's an order here, and it's important. In Doctrine and Covenants, it says, "Signs follow those that believe" (Doctrine and Covenants 63:9). Have a little faith and go slay that giant!

But since we are on the topic of David, let's look forward a little bit in David's life. He had faith that his rock would kill Goliath. He exercised that faith and became not only the hero of that war but the king of the nation. Everything was going so well for David, right?

Well, something happened to David. David took off his breastplate of righteousness for a little while when he decided to start watching Bathsheba bathe on a neighboring rooftop. I wonder if Satan didn't chuckle a little to himself here. *Wait, what? This guy, who was so full of faith and power that he took down a giant, is going to be taken down by this? Really? Wow. I thought I was going to have to try harder than that.*

President Ezra Taft Benson said, "Some of the greatest battles we will face will be fought within the silent chambers of our own souls. David's battles in the field against the foe were not as critical as David's battles in the palace against a lustful eye."[62]

We could go on and on about all of the other stops that Satan will throw at us to derail us from our potential. But for the time being, just remember this story. The little guy kills the big giant. The hero becomes king. King starts looking at things he shouldn't. King's whole life derails as he tries to make that woman his own. Don't let go of the shield of faith!

But here is the kicker in this whole armor description. There is only one weapon. All the armor I have described so far protects us from the adversary's onslaughts. We've got some great protection, but what weapon do we have to fight with?

The last piece that Paul talks about is the sword of the spirit, which is the *word of God*.

> Yea, we see that whosoever will may lay hold upon the word of God, which is quick and powerful, which shall divide asunder all the cunning and the snares and the wiles of the devil, and lead the man of Christ in a strait and narrow course over the gulf of misery and endless woe (Helaman 3:29).

Whosoever will. It's up to us. We can choose to pick up the sword or not. This is where Elder Anderson's definition of faith comes into play. We have to choose to believe that the word of God has the power not only to lead our lives but to protect us from harm. We have to first believe that looking can save us—and that's hard.

Our current prophet, Russell M. Nelson, said:

My dear brothers and sisters, I promise that as you prayerfully study the Book of Mormon every day, you will make better decisions—every day. I promise that as you ponder what you study, the windows of heaven will open, and you will receive answers to your own questions and direction for your own life. I promise that as you daily immerse yourself in the Book of Mormon, you can be immunized against the evils of the day, even the gripping plague of pornography and other mind-numbing addictions.[63]

Immunized against the evils of the day. That's what we need. We need to be inoculated against the power of Satan every day because Satan is constantly changing the strain of the infection. But know this, my friends, Satan's power against us is marginal if we cling to the word of God and to our Savior, Jesus Christ. Think back to the very beginning in the Garden of Eden. Satan was given the power to bruise our heel, but we were given the power to bruise his head (Gen. 3:15).

I see it like this: when I partner with God and pick up the sword of the word of God, Satan can come along like a tiny, little garden snake and bite my heel. Ouch! But I can turn and stomp his head.

I have the power to stomp his head. Unfortunately, though, he doesn't come after my heel just once. It's like I live in the movie *Raiders of the Lost Ark*, and the floor is constantly covered with a multitude of Satan's snakes. There's going to be a lot trying to bite me, and I'm going to have to do a lot of stomping. But God promised our first mother Eve and promised all of us multiple times throughout the scriptures that as we turn to Lord for clarity and guidance, Satan isn't ever going to beat us. He's just not.

And that makes him one angry snake!

About nine years ago, I remember grumbling to myself one night as I prepared for bed. "Why does this keep happening?"

I finished brushing my teeth just a little too hard and then threw my toothpaste back into the drawer louder than was necessary.

We had just returned from dinner with some friends. During the course of dinner, it had come up that a man and woman in our ward had decided to leave the church and take all of their kids with them. All their names were wiped from the records. Every single one.

More and more of my friends and relatives were walking away from the faith we had enjoyed as children and were now navigating this life without organized religion—and what's more, the majority of them had left God and Christ altogether. Here was one more strong family following suit. My emotions were all over the place. They bounced between mad and just so, so sad.

As I entered my closet to grab my pajamas to get ready for bed, I heard a sentence so clear in my mind it could have been a voice. It said, "Melanie if you do not read the Book of Mormon every day, you will follow them out."

I honestly laughed. In retort in my mind, I countered, "Do you know me, Heavenly Father? I'm so full of faith. I go to my meetings and pray and fast and love Jesus and all the things. I would NEVER leave."

But that sentence was repeated again as clearly as I heard it the first time.

"If you do not read the Book of Mormon every day, you'll follow them out."

Over the next few days, I let those words sink in. *Could it be true? Would it be possible for me to lose my faith?* It seemed impossible.

"No way!"

"There is no ... possible ... way."

"Is there a way?"

You may think, like I did, that your faith is strong and that nothing could ever persuade you to leave.

Look around.

I guarantee you know someone who has left that you would never have imagined.

How did it happen?

There are lots of things that cause people to lose their faith. I get it. This life is hard, and we all have a lot of hard things happen to us. Satan is also relentless in his pursuit against goodness and truth. He is so tricky and good at what he does.

We read in 2 Nephi that the devil, "leadeth them away carefully down to hell" (2 Nephi 28:21). Do you know what that scripture and, even more specifically, that word *carefully* means? He's not going to bust in and make me go on a drinking rampage or go murder my neighbor. Satan may not convince you to cheat on your husband or rob a bank. But day by day, he will cunningly whisper in our ears convincing lies that we will begin to believe if we aren't ever diligent in returning to the word of God every single day. He's going to try to trick us all the time.

President Nelson counseled, "If we are to have any hope of sifting through the myriad of voices and the philosophies of men that attack truth, we must learn to receive revelation."[64]

I've taught you this soul-saving, tried and true method for learning to hear the Savior's voice. Now it's up to you. What are you going to do?

I felt over and over during the years of doing the podcast like the character Sam-I-am in the Dr. Seuss book, *Green Eggs and Ham*. In that book, Sam-I-am keeps trying to persuade this guy to eat green eggs and ham. The creature continues to refuse throughout the whole book. Sam-I-am keeps giving him all these opportunities, even the opportunity to eat them in a box with a fox. Still, the creature refuses. Sam-I-am just won't let up. He even follows him underwater.

Sam-I-am is relentless.

Finally, in desperation, and to get Sam-I-am off his back, he concedes. This creature then takes a bite. He quickly discovers that he likes green eggs and ham. Why had he waited so long?

Green Eggs and Ham wraps up with this guy telling everyone how much he likes this new meal and all the places he's going to eat it. On the very last page, he is standing with an empty plate and his arm around Sam-I-am and thanks him over and over.

Don't be like the stubborn guy in the story! Believe me when I say this system works. Believe me when I say the Lord wants to communicate with you. Believe me when I say that Satan wants to deceive you, and it's so gravely important to learn to hear the voice of the Lord right now.

If I could, I would follow you all over the world and offer this gift to you in every place and way I could because I know how delicious the word of the Lord can become to you. You will love it. Just try it.

I'm sure you'll even love it in a box with a fox.*

---

*That's not true. It just sounded good. I've been to Bearizona many, many times, and the fox cage smells the worst. It's so bad. Don't read in a box with a fox. It will sour the experience.

CHAPTER 24

"Did not our heart burn within us, while he talked with us by the way and while he opened to us the scriptures?"

Luke 24:32

I want to end with the story of Christ on the road to Emmaus found in the book of Luke. Mary Magdalene and others are going to the tomb and find it empty. They then see an angel who tells them that Christ has been resurrected. Mary runs and tells the disciples, and initially, they didn't believe her.

Then it says that two disciples are walking to a town called Emmaus. The resurrected Savior shows up and starts walking with them. It says their eyes were "holden that they should not know him" (Luke 24:16). This means they could not tell who He was for some reason.

The Savior asks them why they are sad, and they reply something like this, "For real? Are you a stranger here? Haven't you heard of Jesus? They killed Him a few days ago, and now some ladies say they saw Him, but we haven't seen Him."

Then Christ does something interesting. It says that He starts with Moses and the other prophets and "expounded unto them in all the scriptures the things concerning himself" (Luke 24:27).

They walk a little further and enjoy His company so much that when He turns to leave, they invite Him to have dinner with them. Christ agrees. He sits with them and then breaks bread, blesses it, and gives it to them, and their eyes are opened. They understand that this man they've been with all afternoon is Jesus the Christ. Then the Savior vanishes.

These disciples turn and say to each other, "Did not our heart burn within us, while he talked with us by the way and while he opened to us the scriptures?" (Luke 24:32).

Why do you think the Savior shut their eyes so they would not recognize Him and then came and read the scriptures to them? What a strange thing to do.

I think it was sweet, tender mercy. I believe that Jesus was showing them that they could feel His love and that burning in their hearts simply from listening to the word of God. Christ knew the power of His words and what the Holy Ghost can help us *feel* as we listen to them. He may have been saying, "I won't always be with you, but My word will be. The scriptures have the power to help you feel My love. When you read them, your hearts will burn as the spirit testifies of truth." I think He was saying, "When you miss Me, read about Me in the scriptures. I will be near."

About a month before my divorce was final, my family and I went on a cruise to Mexico. All of us were there except one niece on a mission and my soon-to-be ex-husband. There were over twenty grandkids, my mom, my siblings, and their spouses. We had been planning this trip for the last year and finally, it was here. Before we had decided to divorce, my ex-husband and I had even splurged to the upgraded room with a balcony. It was going to be so great!

Except it wasn't great. When I got to that big ole' room, with the sliding door which led to our own balcony, and a bathroom bigger than a blue port-o-potty, I sat down all alone and started to cry. The tears just wouldn't stop. "How can this be my life?" After twenty-three years of marriage, I was on the brink of being alone.

I cautiously stumbled around the first day, trying to put on a happy face for my family and my kids. Why did I say, "and my kids"? Like I saw them. I didn't. They ran the ship with their cousins, found all the places to hide, and ate all the ice cream cones they could serve themselves.

I hadn't seen some of my siblings in some time, so it was good to sit around and reconnect, play cards, and reminisce. I love my siblings and their spouses, and it is always fun to be with them. But once again, on the inside, I was just so, so sad.

We all met up for dinner that first night, and after the kids tried snails and ordered two or three desserts a piece, they again took off, and everyone separated, heading back to rooms to prepare for a show or something else later that evening. I walked into my room, and once again, it was just too quiet. All that loneliness bounced around my room, like the balls I was sure my kids were hurling at each other up on deck 9. The silence was deafening. I had to leave.

I grabbed my phone and headed to the front of the ship to sit alone on a cluster of vacant deck chairs. Of course, there wasn't Wi-Fi, but it didn't matter—I hadn't gone there to play a game or get on social media. I wanted to speak to my Father in Heaven. I wanted to hear the words of Jesus Christ whispered in my ear. I wanted that comfort and direction I had come to rely on found only in the pages of holy scripture. I opened my phone and began to read, right where I was. I didn't look up "almost single mother of five" in the topical guide.

I was in Alma 25, and as I taught you, I took some notes that night while I read and pondered. The history of this chapter isn't significant, but a few verses jumped out at me. In verse 16, it says in part, "... [the law of Moses did serve to] strengthen their faith in Christ; and thus they did retain a hope through faith, unto eternal salvation, relying upon the spirit of prophecy, which spake of those things to come" (Alma 25:16).

This is what I wrote that night, in the dark on the front of that ship.

"Things to come. I have faith that the Lord is promising me good things. He just promised me a multiplicity of blessings the other day as I was reading and found the answer about the house. But I'm just really sad right now. I'm all alone, and it sucks."

I continued reading. The very next verse ended this way. "... Seeing that the Lord had granted unto them according to their prayers, and he had also verified his word unto them in every particular" (Alma 25:17). When I read those words, my whole body was filled with light, warmth, and love. As I type this, I am filled with the same peace and love I felt that night. Jesus Christ, through the power of the Holy Ghost, pointed directly at me and said with conviction, *I verify My word, Melanie! If I promised you a multiplicity of blessings and everything would be ok, you can bet it will be. I am Jesus Christ. My Father and I only want what is best for you, and We are watching, and We will verify all that We've said and promised you in every particular.*

I wrote this in my notes on the app that night. *"Right after I write good things are going to happen, I read that His word was verified in every particular. He will bless and consecrate this new life. I know it! And it won't be without tears in the meantime. I can wait. I can wait and look forward to ten years down the road to see his plan."*

This may not seem spectacular, but it was just what I needed that night. I needed the reassurance that everything would be ok and that I could do this and move forward all alone. But not all alone, right? I knew that heaven was close and that my Heavenly Father and Jesus Christ were right there with me and would be there for the long haul. I truly wasn't alone and never will be. Like those apostles who walked with Christ and didn't even know it, my heart too burned as I heard His voice through the scriptures. I, too, felt all the love, peace, and calm that comes from walking with Him, listening to Him, and trusting in the means that God gave us to communicate with Him.

I want you to imagine me linking arms with President Nelson and saying this right by his side. I feel the exact same way. "Whenever I hear anyone, including myself, say, 'I know the Book of Mormon is true,' I want to exclaim, 'That's nice, but it is not enough!' We need to feel, deep in 'the inmost part' of our hearts, that the Book of Mormon is unequivocally the word of God. We must feel it so deeply that we would never want to live even one day without it. I might paraphrase President Brigham Young in saying, 'I wish I had the voice of seven thunders to wake up the people' to the truth and power of the Book of Mormon."[65]

As you've read my thoughts, I hope you have felt a little thunder. I hope that deep in your heart, the Spirit bore witness that I'm speaking the truth. I hope you start studying this way and start to understand, in very real ways, how the Savior feels about you. I hope that you develop a love for the Book of Mormon and the scriptures that causes you not to want to live even one day without them.

EPILOGUE

In chapter 19, I told you that four out of five of my kids no longer believe in God or attend church. I need to amend that statement.

In February of 2022, I was studying my scriptures and somehow ended up in Leviticus chapter 25. The following are from my notes from that day.

Leviticus chapter 25

V 8, And thou shalt number seven sabbaths of years unto thee, seven times seven years; and the space of the seven sabbaths of years shall be unto thee forty and nine years. *(That's me right now! Forty-nine!)*

Then shalt thou cause the trumpet of the jubilee to sound on the tenth *day* of the seventh month, in the day of atonement shall ye make the trumpet sound throughout all your land. *(That will be the 10th of July.)*

And ye shall hallow the fiftieth year, and proclaim liberty throughout *all* the land unto all the inhabitants thereof: it shall be a jubilee unto you; and ye shall return every man unto his

possession, and ye shall return every man unto
his family. A jubilee shall that fiftieth year be
unto you.

*So much spirit! So many tears. That seems like a pretty
cool day! Is that the day to shoot for the book to be
done? What is that day? I don't know, but the fiftieth
year being a jubilee year and proclaiming liberty, etc.—
That's the coolest thing ever!!"*

I then read,

Isaiah chapter 61 verses 1 and 9:

The Spirit of the Lord God *is* upon me; because
the Lord hath anointed me to preach good tid-
ings unto the meek; he hath sent me to bind
up the brokenhearted, to proclaim liberty to the
captives, and the opening of the prison to *them
that are* bound;

...And their seed shall be known among the
Gentiles, and their offspring among the people:
all that see them shall acknowledge them that
they *are* the seed *which* the Lord hath blessed."

*Someone who listens to my podcast wrote to me the
other day and said that the Lord will surely bless my
children because of the hard work I'm doing in proclaiming the gospel to so many every week. My kids are
going to be strong and amazing, and the world will
see that blessing that was upon them!*

Because of the Spirit, I felt while studying the scriptures that day, and knowing something great needed to happen on July 10, I decided that I would make that date the hard due date for this book. I had put off finishing it forever, and I needed to just get it done. After I set that date, I studied and prayed, wrote and prayed. I really struggled. "I'm a speaker, not a writer, Heavenly Father." "This is so hard for me!" "I don't want to write this." I even bargained, "If I do this for You, please bless my children. Please."

I didn't tell anyone about the date except Shane and my publisher. My kids certainly had no idea I was even shooting for that day.

As the 10th of July loomed near, I really doubled down. I spent the last few days leading up to the 10th writing around the clock. Around 11 p.m. on July 10th, I hit the wall. I started to cry. I was spent. I couldn't write another word. I was sooo close! I knew I only had a few hours of work left. I wanted to finish it by that special day. It was the beginning of the jubilee, remember? But I could not write another word, so I went to bed and decided I would finish it in the morning.

I got up, determined to complete it. After a few more hours, I typed, "The End." I can't clearly describe the emotion that filled my soul. I felt like Jesus and I gave each other a big high-five. It was finally done.

Later that morning, I got a call from my oldest son—the boy who once pointed his finger in my face and said that he would never believe in The Church of Jesus Christ of Latter-day Saints. **What he told**

me in that phone call is the crown of this whole book and the start of my jubilee year. It validates all I have said. It is another testimony of the power that Christ has to use the Book of Mormon to soften our hearts and help us feel His love and be converted. I so wish I would have finished on the 10th and not the 11th. It would have made the story just that much cooler. But that's on me and my procrastination. The Lord was on time with His promise.

I was hoping I could get my son to recount his story, but he hasn't had the time. I will give the cliff notes version. Long story short, he fell in love with a good, shiny, amazing, bright, returned missionary. He started going back to church with her and was doing all the right things but couldn't get past some of the information he'd been told about church history and other things that bothered him. He wasn't feeling it. He tried for six months. Finally, he was challenged by his girlfriend's prior mission president to read the Book of Mormon in six-weeks time. He said no. After that, he felt like he needed to break up with her. He just wasn't the guy she wanted. She wanted a temple marriage, and he didn't. They were just too different.

Luckily, he changed his mind about reading the Book of Mormon. *What could it hurt?* he thought. This girl was too great, and he now loved her too much to just give up without giving it this last try. He began listening to the Book of Mormon every night at work while he cleaned carpets. (He didn't even know you could speed it up the talking. I can't listen to anything at normal speed!) It took him two weeks to finish it. He had a special experience one night while listening that led him to believe that there was a God, which then led him to more purpose-ful prayers. But it wasn't until the night he finished it that his answer came. As he sat pondering about the church the night he finished it, he was led to a website that helped him see that someone could come back to the church, even if they had concerns or questions. He felt the Spirit testify that he could do it.

After reading an article on the website, he slid out of bed and onto his knees. He told me that he prayed the most purposeful prayer he has ever ut-tered. He told the Lord that he needed to know this was the place that God wanted him to be. He needed to know that God wanted him to return to The Church of Jesus Christ of Latter-day Saints and be an active member again. Then he told the Lord, "And I need to know in an undeniable way."

He got off his knees and decided to open his paper scriptures instead of reading on his phone. I had spoken so many times that the Lord uses the scriptures to answer our prayers. He decided to try it. He pulled his dusty quad down off the bookcase. I don't think he'd opened it once in the last seven or eight years. He flipped it open and just put his finger down on a page.

His finger landed on Doctrine and Covenants 75, verse 12, which read, "Behold, this is the will of the Lord your God concerning you. Even so. Amen" (Doctrine and Covenants 75:12).

He said that a feeling came over him that he had never felt before. He now knows that it was the Spir-it of the Lord answering his prayer through the power of the Holy Ghost. His whole body felt the power of that answer. He knew it came from God.

He explained to me that he used to think there was only one way of knowing something. Now he knows that isn't true. He said that of course we do need to use our minds and logic, and God wants and expects us to do that. But He also wants us to open our hearts to *feel* His love and confirmation of the truth. He wants us to not only hear but also to *feel* His love. This way of knowing was something he never knew existed before.

I believe that listening to the Book of Mormon for so many hours every day softened his heart to the point that he was ready to receive God's will for him. It let him know that God is real and led him to a direct answer he needed to move forward.

Does he still have questions? Yes. Are there things that still bother him? Yes. But his faith is strong in what he does know. He feels the Spirit every day. He's so happy. He looks like a different kid. He recently got ordained a priest, has been to the temple to do baptisms, and received his patriarchal blessing. I received a text a few weeks after his experience with the scriptures that said, "I wish I would have listened to you earlier about the church. The past few weeks I have felt so much happiness and peace that I never knew I was missing. It's super awesome." And a few weeks ago he was ordained an Elder. He and his fiancée are planning on being sealed in the temple in the spring.

THERE ARE NO WORDS TO DESCRIBE MY JOY.

He's a little worried that people won't believe him. He thinks people will think he came back to the church to get the girl. And that's ok. I will ever be grateful for that shiny, amazing girlfriend for not giving in and settling for less than an eternal union. She was a shining light that lit his path back to Jesus. He wouldn't have gotten to the place where he picked up the Book of Mormon had it not been for her. But in the end, it wasn't the girl who convinced him that this is the place that the Lord wants him to be. Jesus Christ is the one who stepped in and answered that prayer. Through the power of the Holy Ghost, Heavenly Father, and Jesus Christ let him know as clearly as if they had spoken to him directly that this is the place for him and that he will do great work in the church and in his family in the future.

If people criticize him and tell him he's back just to get the girl, he can shrug his shoulders and remember what President Nelson recently said, "Regardless of what others may say or do, no one can ever take away a witness borne to your heart and mind about what is true."[66]

You see, all I've said works. It worked for my son. It changed his heart. Turning to the scriptures let the Spirit speak to him in an undeniable way. He's back. He's full of the Spirit. He's preparing to be sealed to his wife for eternity. The Book of Mormon brought my boy back to Jesus. It's the biggest miracle.

The majority of my kids still don't believe. But its ok. I love them and see all the good they are offering to this world. I have faith. Whether in this life or maybe even in the next, that truth will find its way back to them.

You parents out there, who worry every day about your kids, just know that Heavenly Father and Jesus

Christ love them even more than you do. Let's keep praying, hoping, and loving these kids. Let's look at all the good they are doing and never stop loving them. Let's look to the Savior to ease our worry as we wait. Turn to the scriptures for comfort and direction. Let the Lord heal your heart and ease your burdens through the power of His word. Remember, truth will always find a way.

*If you want to hear my son's conversion story in his own words, please listen to Season 4, Episode 33 of my podcast, Come Follow Me For Us. It is titled, "My Son's Conversion Story."

**For current information, to listen to the podcast, or to share your feelings with Melanie, please visit www.melaniewstroud.com

ACKNOWLEDGMENTS

There are so many people to thank, and I'm sure I forgot you. I'm sorry. Please know I just shot up in bed and said, "Oh no! I forgot (insert your name)." My busy brain is no good at remembering all I should remember. Blame my brain and not me. It seems like they aren't working together much anymore.

I want to start by thanking my sister-in-law Tami Gordon. Thanks for dropping that book into my lap so many years ago and for believing I could influence the world in the same sort of way. You lit a fire in me that has yet to be extinguished. I love you.

I want to thank my mom, Chris Price, for being my lifelong cheerleader. Whenever I called and read her a chapter, she spilled out all the "gush" I talked about in this book. She made me think that I was the best writer in the world. I'm grateful for the golden carrot she dangled in front of me and for taking this writing thing of mine seriously. Her generosity and faith in me helped make this miracle happen. I'm so grateful for the faith-filled life she has lived and for her courage and example. We lost our dad way too young, and she has done the parenting for both of them for a very long time. I'm sure my dad is as proud of her as I am.

I'm thankful for my sweet husband, Shane. While I wrote, he never let much time pass without bringing me a sandwich, a treat, or ensuring I was well hydrated. (What's his deal with hydration? Haha) He's always so encouraging and kind. I know he's a special gift to me from a loving Heavenly Father. I love him so much. BTW, he just noticed me crying as I wrote this, grabbed a tissue, and came and somewhat aggressively wiped my whole face. He makes me laugh so hard. He's so good to me. How did I get so lucky?

I'm thankful for my sister Shelby Stroud and my most favorite friend, Emily Crowton. These girls are the ones that talk Jesus with me all the day long. They constantly testify of truth as they see it in their lives. They are great examples of living the gospel and loving Jesus. And we laugh—hard. I'm glad we don't pay for long distance by the minute like our parents did. We'd be broke.

I'm grateful for my kids, who encouraged me to write and expressed confidence that I could actually get this done. They have all been generous with their praise that I could accomplish such a huge thing. I love them. I am proud of the great kids they are and all they offer this world. I'm grateful every day that I get to be their mother.

I'm thankful for those I love who are now on the other side. I'm grateful for my dad, Ron Price, who always taught me to look to the Lord. I'm thankful for the powerful lesson he taught our family about trusting God and not giving in to bitterness when things don't go the way we want. I have felt him near often in my life. I miss him more than words can say.

I'm grateful for my grandparents, my ex-husband's dad, Bruce Wellman, my dear mission companion, Yuko, and my sister-in-law Brittany Atkinson. I know they are not far from my family and me. The Book of Mormon testifies that angels whisper the words of Christ. I know these people I love still play a part in inspiring my children and me. I know Brittany has been close to my Chandler this past year. She was a doer, and I imagine she hit the ground running on the other side when she left us on Christmas Day 2021. Has it already been a whole year?

I'm grateful for all of you who have listened to the podcast and written words of encouragement to me over the years. Without you, I wouldn't have had the guts to put pen to paper and send my actual written words out to the world. You taught me that my unique voice was needed. You gave me the confidence to keep talking, even when I felt I didn't have much to say. Thanks for laughing at my crazy and following my tangents to the end. You are my people. And a special thanks to those who supported me through Patreon for years. You allowed me to love and marry someone in another state. Without you, I would be loveless and sad. You blessed my life for a long time. Thank you so much!

Thanks to all the beta readers who took the time to trudge through the book while it was still a mess. I appreciate your time, patience, and very thoughtful suggestions. I hope you are reading a free copy of the book. If not, haha, sucker, you should have asked for one.

I'm thankful for Blair Parke, my editor, who took all my terrible grammar and reckless use of too

many different tenses and turned them into a cohesive manuscript that I am proud of. It was quite
the task. Thanks also for advising me to take out so
many exclamation points. I see now that I sounded
like a super peppy psycho! Which I'm not! Phew!
Glad we straightened that out!! I'm so grateful for
her!!

And last, I'm beyond thankful for my publisher,
Chloe Simons. I'm so grateful that she listened to the
promptings of the Spirit and reached out to me so
long ago. If it weren't for her, this book would still
be a jumbled mess in my mind and little pieces on
the computer. I will forever be grateful to her for
getting this message to the world. I wish her every
success with her publishing company, E n' S Publishing, and in her life. She deserves it. I hope that for
every person touched by the words in this book, she
gets another point in heaven—a pass for a swear,
a Diet Coke, or whatever we get in heaven for helping people reach their potential here. I hope she gets
a lot of whatever that is. She's the best.

ENDNOTES

1   President Russell M Nelson, "Revelation for the Church, Revelation for our Lives," The Church of Jesus Christ of Latter-day Saints online, April 2018, https://www.churchofjesuschrist.org/study/general-conference/2018/04/revelation-for-the-church-revelation-for-our-lives?lang=eng

2   President Thomas S. Monsoon, "The Power of the Book of Mormon," The Church of Jesus Christ of Latter-day Saints online, April 2017, https://www.churchofjesuschrist.org/study/general-conference/2017/04/the-power-of-the-book-of-Mormon?lang=eng

3   "Joseph Smith—History: Extracts from The History of Joseph Smith, the Prophet," Chapter 1:12, Pearl of Great Price, The Church of Jesus Christ of Latter-day Saints online, October 21, 2022, https://www.churchofjesuschrist.org/study/scriptures/pgp/js-h/1?lang=eng

4   President Ezra Taft Benson, "The Book of Mormon-The Keystone of Our Religion," The Church of Jesus Christ of Latter-day Saints online, October 1986, https://www.churchofjesuschrist.org/study/general-conference/1986/10/the-book-of-Mormon-the-keystone-of-our-religion?lang=eng

5 "Introduction to the Book of Mormon," The Church of Jesus Christ of Latter-day Saints online, October 21, 2022, https://www.churchofjesuschrist.org/study/scriptures/bofm/introduction?lang=eng

6 Joy D. Jones, "An Especially Noble Calling," The Church of Jesus Christ of Latter-day Saints online, April 2020, https://www.churchofjesuschrist.org/study/general-conference/2020/04/14jones?lang=eng

7 Webster Dictionary 1913 Online, s.v. "counsel," accessed October 25, 2022, https://www.dictionary.com/browse/counsel

8 Elder Marcus Nash "And Out of Weakness He Shall be Made Strong," Devotionals, BYU Idaho, accessed October 25, 2022, http://www.byui.edu/devotionals/elder-marcus-b-nash

9 Elder Richard G. Scott, "Using the Supernal Gift of Prayer," The Church of Jesus Christ of Latter-day Saints online, April 2007, https://www.churchofjesuschrist.org/study/general-conference/2007/04/using-the-supernal-gift-of-prayer?lang=eng

10 Elder Gary E. Stevenson, "Look to the Book, Look to the Lord," The Quorum of the Twelve Apostles, The Church of Jesus Christ of Latter-day Saints online, November 2016, https://www.churchofjesuschrist.org/study/ensign/2016/11/saturday-afternoon-session/look-to-the-book-look-to-the-lord?lang=eng

11 Elder Douglas D Holmes, "Deep in our Hearts," The Church of Jesus Christ of Latter-day Saints online, April 2020, https://www.churchofjesuschrist.org/study/general-conference/2020/04/16holmes?lang=eng

12 Children's Songbook 109, "Search, Ponder, and Pray," The Church of Jesus Christ of Latter-day Saints online, accessed October 25, 2022, https://www.churchofjesuschrist.org/music/library/childrens-songbook/search-ponder-and-pray?lang=eng

13 Elder Boyd K. Packer, "These Things I Know," The Church of Jesus Christ of Latter-day Saints online, April 2013, https://www.churchofjesuschrist.org/study/general-conference/2013/04/these-things-I-know?lang=eng

14 President Thomas S. Monson, "The Power of the Book of Mormon," The Church of Jesus Christ of Latter-day Saints online, April 2017 Ensign, https://www.churchofjesuschrist.org/study/general-conference/2017/04/the-power-of-the-book-of-mormon?lang=eng

15 Elder Dallin H. Oaks, "Good, Better, Best," The Church of Jesus christ of Latter-day Saints online, October 2007, https://www.churchofjesuschrist.org/study/general-conference/2017/10/good-better-best?lang=eng

16 Old Testament 2022 Manual, "Using Come Follow Me- For Individuals and Families," Resource Page, The Church of Jesus Christ of Latter-day Saints online, accessed October 25, 2022, https://www.churchofjesuschrist.org/study/manual/come-follow-me-for-individuals-and-families-old-testament-2022/using?lang=eng

17 President Russell M. Nelson, "Make Time For the Lord," The Church of Jesus Christ of Latter-day Saints online, October 2021, https://

www.churchofjesuschrist.org/study/general-conference/2021/10/59nelson?lang=eng

18 "Teachings of Presidents of the Church: Harold B. Lee" pg. 66, The Church of Jesus Christ of Latter-day Saints online, 2000, https://www.churchofjesuschrist.org/study/manual/teachings-of-presidents-harold-b-lee?lang=eng

19 Howard W. Hunter, "Reading the Scriptures," The Church of Jesus Christ of Latter-day Saints online, November 1979, https://www.churchofjesuschrist.org/study/ensign/1979/11/reading-the-scriptures?lang=eng

20 Elder Richard G. Scott, "Using the Supernal Gift of Prayer," The Church of Jesus Christ of Latter-day Saints online, April 2007, https://www.churchofjesuschrist.org/study/general-conference/2007/04/using-the-supernal-gift-of-prayer?lang=eng

21 Elder Richard G. Scott, "Make the Exercise of Faith Your First Priority," The Church of Jesus Christ of Latter-day Saints online, October 2014, https://www.churchofjesuschrist.org/study/general-conference/2014/10/make-the-exercise-of-faith-your-first-priority?lang=eng

22 2020 Youth Theme Song, "Go and Do," The Church of Jesus Christ of Latter-Day Saints online, accessed October 25, 2022, https://www.churchofjesuschrist.org/youth/childrenandyouth/youth-theme-2020?lang=eng

23 Elder Ronald A Rasband, "Behold! I am a God of Miracles," The Church of Jesus Christ of Latter-day Saints online, April 2021, https://

www.churchofjesuschrist.org/study/general-confer-ence/2021/04/52rasband?lang=eng

24 Elder Dale G. Renlund, "Repentance: A Joyful Choice," The Church of Jesus Christ of Latter-day Saints online, October 2016, https://www.churchofjesuschrist.org/study/general-confer-ence/2016/10/repentance-a-joyful-choice?lang=eng

25 Lawrence Corbridge, "Stand Forever," Speeches, BYU online, January 22, 2019, https://speeches.byu.edu/talk/lawrence-e-corbridge/stand-for-ever

26 President Ezra Taft Benson, "The Book of Mormon—Keystone of Our Religion," The Church of Jesus Christ of Latter-day Saints, November 1986, https://www.churchofjesuschrist.org/study/en-sign/1986/11/the-book-of-mormon-keystone-of-our-re-ligion?lang=eng&id=p14#p14

27 Marvin J. Ashton, "There are Many Gifts," The Church of Jesus Christ of Latter-day Saints on-line, October 1987, https://www.churchofjesuschrist.org/study/general-conference/1987/10/there-are-many-gifts?lang=eng

28 President Thomas S. Monson, "The Power of the Book of Mormon," The Church of Jesus Christ of Latter-day Saints online, April 2017, https://www.churchofjesuschrist.org/study/general-conference/the-power-of-the-book-of-mormon?lang=eng

29 President Russell M. Nelson, "The Book of Mormon: What Would Your Life Be Like with-out It?" Ensign, The Church of Jesus Christ of Latter-day Saints online, November 2017, https://

www.churchofjesuschrist.org/study/general-conference/2017/10/the-book-of-mormon-what-would-your-life-be-like-without-it?lang=eng

30 John H. Groberg, "Writing Your Personal and Family History, General Conference, The Church of Jesus Christ of Latter-day Saints, April 1980, https://www.churchofjesuschrist.org/study/general-conference/1980/04/writing-your-personal-and-family-history?lang=eng

31 Dallin H. Oaks, "Our Strengths can Become our Downfall," Brigham Young University-Provo Fireside, Speeches, BYU.edu, June 7, 1992, https://speeches.byu.edu/talks/dallin-h-oaks/strengths-can-become-downfall

32 Elder Neil L. Anderson, "Faith is Not by Chance, but by Choice," The Church of Jesus Christ of Latter-day Saints online, November 2015, https://www.churchofjesuschrist.org/study/general-conference/2015/10/faith-is-not-by-chance-but-by-choice?lang=eng

33 Elder Marcus B. Nash, "And Out of Weakness He Shall Be Made Strong" Brigham Young University-Idaho Devotional, November 12, 2013, https://www.byui.edu/devotionals/elder-marcus-b-nash

34 "Introduction to the Book of Mormon," The Church of Jesus Christ of Latter-day Saints online, accessed October 28, 2022, https://www.churchofjesuschrist.org/study/scripture/bofm/introduction?lang=eng

35 President Russell M. Nelson, "The Book of Mormon: What Would Your Life Be Like without

It?" The Church of Jesus Christ of Latter-day Saints online, October 2017, https://www.churchofjesuschrist.org/study/general-conference/2017/10/the-book-of-mormon-what-would-your-life-be-like-without-it?lang=eng

36 President Russel M. Nelson, "Come Follow Me," The Church of Jesus Christ of Latter-day Saints online, April 2019, https://www.churchofjesuschrist.org/study/general-conference/2019/04/46nelson?lang=eng

37 Elder Marcus B. Nash, "And Out of Weakness He Shall Be Made Strong," BYU Idaho Devotional, BYU Idaho online, November 12, 2013, https://www.byui.edu/devotionals/elder-marcus-b-nash

38 Elder Bednar, "Clean Hands and Pure Hearts," The Church of Jesus Christ of Latter-day Saints online, October 2007, www.churchofjesuschrist.org/study/general-conference/2007/10/clean-hands-and-pure-hearts?lang=eng

39 President Russell M. Nelson, "The Book of Mormon: What Would Your Life Be Like without It?" The Church of Jesus Christ of Latter-day Saints online, October 2017, https://www.churchofjesuschrist.org/study/general-conference/2017/10/the-book-of-mormon-what-would-your-life-be-like-without-it?lang=eng

40 Ibid

41 Elder David A Bednar "In the Strength of the Lord" Brigham Young University–Idaho online, October 23, 2001, https://speeches.byu.edu/talks/david-a-bednar/strength-lord

42 Ibid

43 Elder Benjamin M. Tai, "The Power of the Book of Mormon in Conversion," The Church of Jesus Christ of Latter-day Saints online, April 2020, https://www.churchofjesuschrist.org/study/general-conference/2020/04/27tai?lang=eng

44 "Faith," Children's Songbook, The Church of Jesus Christ of Latter-day Saints online, pg. 96, accessed October 29, 2022, https://www.churchofjesuschrist.org/music/library/childrens-songbook/faith?lang=eng

45 Jeffery R. Holland, "Lord, I Believe," General Conference, The Church of Jesus Christ of Latter-day Saints online, April 2013, https://www.churchofjesuschrist.org/study/general-conference/2013/04/lord-i-believe?lang=eng

46 Matthew J. Grow, "The Extraordinary Life of Parley P. Pratt, Autobiography, pg. 20, The Church of Jesus Christ of Latter-day Saints online, April 2007, https://www.churchofjesuschrist.org/study/ensign/2007/04/the-extraordinary-life-of-parley-p-pratt?lang=eng

47 Elder M. Russell Ballard, "Be Strong in the Lord," The Church of Jesus Christ of Latter-day Saints online, July 2004, https://www.churchofjesuschrist.org/study/ensign/2004/07/be-strong-in-the-lord?lang=eng

48 "Joseph Smith History, 1:15-16 Pearl of Great Price," The Church of Jesus Christ of Latter-day Saints online, accessed October 29, 2022, https://www.churchofjesuschrist.org/study/scriptures/pgp/js-h/1?lang=eng

49 "Keep the Commandments," hymn, 303 Hymnbook, The Church of Jesus Christ of Latter-day Saints online, accessed on October 29, 2022, https://www.churchofjesuschrist.org/music/library/hymns/keep-the-commandments?lang=eng

50 Elder M. Russell Ballard, "Here Am I, Send Me," BYU Devotional, Brigham Young University online, March 13, 2001, https://speeches.byu.edu/talks/m-russell-ballard/send/

51 Lawrence Corbridge, "Stand Forever," BYU Speeches, BYU online, January 22, 2019, https://speeches.byu.edu/talks/lawrence-e-corbridge/stand-forever

52 President Russell M. Nelson, "Joy and Spiritual Survival," The Church of Jesus Christ of Latter-day Saints online, October 2016, https://www.churchofjesuschrist.org/study/general-conference/2016/10/joy-and-spiritual survival?lang=eng

53 Webster's 1913 Online, s.v. "manifest," accessed October 29, 2022, https://www.websters1913.com/words/Manifest

54 President Gordon B. Hinckley, "If Ye be Willing and Obedient," The Church of Jesus Christ of Latter-day Saints online, October 1971, https://www.churchofjesuschrist.org/study/general-conference/1971/10/if-ye-be-willing-and-obedient?lang=eng

55 Elder Von G. Keetch, "Blessed and Happy Are Those Who Keep the Commandments of God," The Church of Jesus Christ of Latter-day Saints online, November 2015, https://www.churchofjesuschrist.org/2015/10/blessed-and-happy-are-those-who-keep-the-commandments-of-god?lang=eng

56 Elder Neal A. Maxwell, "Swallowed Up in the Will of the Father," The Church of Jesus Christ of Latter-day Saints online, October 1995, https://www.churchofjesuschrist.org/study/general-conference/1995/10/swallowed-up-in-the-will-of-the-father?lang=eng

57 Wendy Nelson, Church News Podcast, Episode 12, The Church News online, January 2021, https://www.thechurchnews.com/2021/1/5/23265235/sister-wendy-nelson-sheri-dew-president-nelson-prophet-three-years

58 Elder Jeffrey R. Holland, "The Cost—and Blessings—of Discipleship," The Church of Jesus Christ of Latter-day Saints online, April 2014, https://www.churchofjesuschrist.org/study/general-conference/2014/04/the-cost-and-blessings-of-discipleship?lang=eng

59 Elder Ulisses Soares, "Be Meek and Lowly of Heart," The Church of Jesus Christ of Latter-day Saints online, October 2013, https://www.churchofjesuschrist.org/study/general-conference/2013/10/be-meek-and-lowly-of-heart?lang=eng

60 President Wilford Woodruff, Deseret News: Semi-Weekly, January 15, 1883, 1., https://www.churchofjesuschrist.org/study/manual/teachings-wilford-woodruff/chapter-21?lang=eng

61 Elder Neil L. Andersen, "Faith Is Not by Chance, but by Choice," The Church of Jesus Christ of Latter-day Saints online, October 2015, https://www.churchofjesuschrist.org/study/general-conference/2015/10/faith-is-not-by-chance-but-by-choice?lang=eng

62 Ezra Taft Benson, "In His Steps, First Presidency Message," The Church of Jesus Christ of Latter-day Saints online, September 1988, Ensign, https://www.churchofjesuschrist.org/study/ensign/1988/09/in-his-steps?lang=eng

63 President Russell M. Nelson "The Book of Mormon, What Would Your Life Be Like Without It?" The Church of Jesus Christ of Latter-day Saints online, October 2017, https://www.churchofjesuschrist.org/study/general/2017/10/the-book-of-mormon-what-would-your-life-be-like-without-it?lang=eng

64 President Russell M. Nelson, "Revelation for the Church, Revelation for our Lives," The Church of Jesus Christ of Latter-day Saints online, April 2018, https://www.churchofjesuschrist.org/study/general-conference/2018/04/revelation-for-the-church-revelation-for-our-lives?lang=eng

65 President Brigham Young, "The Book of Mormon: What Would Your Life Be Like Without It?," The Church of Jesus Christ of Latter-day Saints online, October 2017, https://www.churchofjesuschrist.org/study/general-conference/20/17/10/the-book-of-mormon-what-would-your-life-be-like-without-it?lang=eng

66 President Russell M. Nelson, "Revelation for the Church, Revelation for Our Lives," The Church of Jesus Christ of Latter-day Saints online, April 2018, https://www.churchofjesuschrist.org/study/general-conference/2018/04/revelation-for-the-church-revelation-for-our-lives?lang=eng

Made in the USA
Columbia, SC
30 November 2023

26887070R00159